Preparing Your Heart for Marriage

Preparing Your Heart for Marriage

Dr. Cassandra Bolar

Preparing Your Heart for Marriage /Cassandra Bolar —1st ed.
ISBN 978-0-578-50005-8

To my dear husband, Dr. Ronnie Bolar: Thank you for your unconditional love that has transformed my life and given me the security to chase my dreams.

Contents

Acknowledgments

I WOULD LIKE TO thank my dear husband, Dr. Ronnie Bolar, for your love and support during the process of birthing this book. Thank you for believing in my calling and helping me overcome my fears. Your unconditional love continues to heal me in ways beyond your imagination. I would also like to thank my parents (David and Jacqueline Kirkland), family, and friends for your unfailing support of my efforts to uplift relationships and marriages. Thank you, Anthony "AJ" Joiner and Katrina Estall, for your professional help with the production of this book. I appreciate your kindness and expertise.

Most of all, I would like to thank my personal Savior, Jesus Christ, for placing this burning desire in my heart to positively impact marriages and families. The relationship with my heavenly Father has taught me so many principles for relationships. I pray that this work is pleasing unto you and helps others achieve the greatness you always had in mind for their marriages and families.

Introduction

Yes, I'm a hopeless romantic, and I love the concept and action of love. I suppose that's why I chose to be a marriage and family therapist. If we truly understood the power of love and its symbiotic relationship with marriage, I don't believe our culture would have a love/hate relationship with marriage. A sense of indifference toward marriage is creeping into our culture. This apathy is a matter of the heart and a reflection of the collective hurt and pain many individuals have encountered in navigating the tricky terrain of love and marriage. Marriage is one of the most conducive environments for the growth and maturity of love. Choice and free will are requirements for romantic love. Even God gives us a choice to love him. We don't choose our own parents or our children, but we do choose our spouse. This unique element of having no biological ties with an individual you choose to love for a lifetime is what makes marriage so special. When we are successful with love on this level, we are successful with a gift God gave to humanity. And success in any area of life requires preparation.

On a basic and simplified level, we use our hearts to love. Love is at the center of a healthy marriage, and the condition of the heart determines how well love is pumped throughout the individuals involved in marriage and the culture they create in their marriage. More specifically, the condition of your heart is the driving force behind the quality of your relational experiences. The regulation of your emotions and thinking is a matter of the heart, which has important implications for marriage. If your heart is unhealed, you will not be able to provide the unconditional love that is required for a healthy marriage. Therefore, preparing the heart for marriage is critical to the success of marriage. That's the whole premise behind this book; you must prepare your heart—your emotions and desires—for a successful marriage. I pray that you will not only see this book as a means for your intellectual stimulation, but I hope that you will also utilize this book as a tool to begin the process of preparing your heart for one of the greatest journeys in life—marriage. OK, now that you know my heart and intentions behind this book, let's dive in.

The Soul Mate Dilemma

I need to address this early because I don't want you to be misconstrued by the predominant perspective on finding and doing life with your soul mate. We live in a culture that wants to take the work out of greatness but expects the rewards of hard work and the building process. Your soul mate isn't someone you find, then your life perfectly aligns. Nor will your marriage be easy because you found the perfect match. Perfection doesn't exist, but excellence is a reality. A soul mate isn't someone you find; a soul mate is someone you become. Each day you are gifted with an opportunity to grow in your capacity to serve as a soul mate to your spouse. This book is all about doing the internal work to prepare yourself to love your spouse on the deepest level possible—beyond the superficial and to the true essence of your partner. This book isn't a how-to guide to find your soul mate. It's more of a guide for conditioning your heart to have the capacity to walk into marriage from a state of wholeness and emotional and spiritual health.

Let's go ahead and simplify the concept of soul mate. Your soul is comprised of your mind, will, and emotions. When preparing to walk into marriage, you want to utilize your mind to make a sober, intelligent decision. We'll delve into factors that can cloud your judgment as we get further into the book. Additionally, the Lord is a gentleman, and he isn't going to force anyone on you. How many of you have heard from someone you were dating say, "The Lord told me you are going to be my wife, or the Lord told me you are going to be my husband"? If you guys broke up, and there is no possibility of you two getting married, well . . . somebody lied, and it wasn't Jesus. You have a will. Opportunities will be presented in your life, and you will have a conscious choice to make when it comes to marriage. You have your own will and sense of agency when it comes to marriage. Your personal will has a decision to make—marriage is too important and affects your life and purpose in critical ways; it can't be a decision that you slide into haphazardly. Lastly, your emotions are extremely powerful; when not harnessed in the right direction, they will try to take over your decision-making. Emotions—in and of themselves—are not bad. God gave us emotions for a reason. However, you don't want the important decision of choosing whom you will marry to be determined completely by feelings and emotions. This decision must be grounded in something more stable than the ever-changing landscape of your emotions. You must submit your emotions and heart to the Lord. In all, he should be at the heart or seated on the throne of what controls your emotions. No one or nothing else should take his place—not even your spouse. This truth and principle to live by will help stabilize your emotions and give you the foundation for building not only a healthy marriage, but healthy relationships in all areas of your life.

Now that we have a basic, simplified understanding of "soul," the meaning of "mate" is 1) *a companion, comrade, or fellow worker;* 2) *one of a pair, especially a matched pair.*[1] You see, before you get paired up with your life partner—your spouse—you want to make sure that your soul is whole. You want certainty that your heart is in a condition as to where you have been a good steward over yourself, and you will be a good steward over the gift of your spouse and the gift of marriage. We all have a keen understanding of what we want from the other person when we get married, but we don't often take an inventory of ourselves to ensure that we are all of what we are looking for in a spouse.

So, let me just tell you where I'm coming from in my approach to this book. I'm coming to you as a healthy marriage advocate. I'm a marriage and family therapist, Christian, researcher and professor, but at my core, I'm a person who believes in the power of love and the sanctity of marriage. I'm packing this book with all I have—my passion, personal experience, research-based information, biblical insights, practical strategies, and professional expertise. This book was birthed out of my calling and my commission. This book isn't about me; it's about you and positively impacting the culture of marriage in our society. Granted, I will unashamedly use some of my personal experiences as illustrations to assist with providing clarity on concepts I bring to bear in this book. However, don't get caught up on me. I'm not perfect or the savviest person in the field, but I have prayed that this message will resonate with you in a way that will assist you in preparing your heart for marriage. I pray this message will be transformative for your outlook and heart toward marriage. More than anything, I want your heart to be postured and conditioned for a healthy marriage. Regardless of the outcome, understand that marriage is a good thing and you have the capacity to prepare for and experience a healthy marriage that honors God and transforms a community.

Purpose of This Book

This book is an effort to improve your performance in marriage so that you will be in the practice of allowing the Holy Spirit to guide you in your relationships, a critical area the enemy tries to use against us. This is not another book about how to become the perfect wife or the perfect husband. It's also not an effort to provide a prescription for the steps to find a spouse, or to devalue individuals who are not married. The message is simple: Marriage is a beautiful institution that was created by God for the well-being of adults, children, and society overall. God honors marriage, and when we take the success of marriage seriously, it demonstrates that we honor marriage as well. This book is about conditioning your heart and making it fertile for the opportunity of marriage. I know you want your marriage to be fruitful and successful, and I do, too. That's why I utilize this book to share the truth with you in love and grace.

Conditioning isn't glamorous. It's the preparation that's done privately that will be rewarded publicly. The preparation for marriage means addressing the hardened places of your heart, breaking up the stony ground of your heart and getting it ready to be successful at marriage. This means going beyond a superficial examination of your heart; you need to go to the deep places. Discover the root causes for your actions, fears, hopes and desires.

Preparing your heart for marriage is so much more than just going to premarital counseling. Most people go to premarital counseling as a means to check off an item on the to-do list for the wedding. No, you need to dig deeper than that. Don't get me wrong, because I'm a huge advocate for premarital counseling, but the preparation I'm talking about is the work you need to do on yourself as an individual before you become a couple.

You want to be a good manager over yourself before you become a steward over a marriage and your spouse. What are some of the habits or perspectives that are detrimental to a healthy marriage that would be important for you to work on before you get married? Now, no one will be perfect before marriage, but there are issues you may need to address within yourself prior to introducing someone else into your life. You don't want your personal challenges to make your spouse's life harder. For example, if you have a hard time with managing money, it would be helpful to yourself, your marriage, and your spouse to begin gaining traction in addressing this issue prior to marriage. The condition of the heart is the root to a bad spending habit, and I will detail ways in which you can successfully address underlying heart issues that drive bad behavior. Working on these heart issues now serves as a preventive measure. Marriage has a way of amplifying heart issues and their potential consequences because those issues aren't just affecting you anymore.

Some people think that the step of getting married will be a panacea for their character flaws; however, marriage won't magically change you into a better person. If you have trouble with faithfulness, it's not going to magically disappear once you get married. You must get to the heart of the issue and address causal factors that may influence your desires and emotions surrounding behaviors that wouldn't be helpful for you in a marriage, or in general for that matter. It could be a host of issues, such as anger, unfaithfulness, unforgiveness, addictions, and so on. This book gets to the heart of the issue by exploring the heart conditions that can potentially drive behaviors that would be detrimental to a marriage. The reality is that we all have work or conditioning we can do to help us perform better in marriage. Just like in sports, all talent levels must go through the conditioning process prior to the sports season, and all players end up performing better than they would have if they had skipped that process.

With this book, I'm not promising that you will get married. However, this book focuses on the internal and spiritual work needed to position your heart and mind in the right place for marriage. Faith without works is dead, and this book focuses on the healing work you can do as an individual to prepare yourself for marriage. It would be unfortunate if the opportunity or the season was fitting to move forward or progress toward marriage came along, but you missed your opportunity because your heart and mind set weren't in the right place. That's where this book comes into play. Opportunities have a way of meeting preparation. It's about turning your heart toward marriage. To avoid making a false god out of marriage, many have denied their desire for marriage. Interestingly, many are trying not to lift-up marriage as a false god in their lives, but they have exalted independence and selfishness instead. We've almost over-spiritualized marriage. I've heard so many people say "Jesus is my husband." Jesus is your savior—not your spouse. There's a fullness in your life that only he can fulfill, and there could be something he wants you to fulfill on earth in which a life partner could be used to help you along with that process. We have free will and choices to make in life. God is not going to twist your arm in any direction, but you want to be sensitive to the Holy Spirit. Remember, the Lord considers marriage as an honorable institution. It's a godly desire. There is such a delicate balance between having an expectant heart for marriage while also maintaining a content heart with singleness. "For I have learned, in whatsoever state I am, therewith to be content" (Phil. 4:11b KJV). Yes, singleness is a gift, and you want to utilize that time wisely. However, if marriage is a desire of your heart, you don't want to secretly deny it and postpone marriage indefinitely. Sure, there is a time and season for everything, but there is a time limit on some opportunities in life.

What you do want to be concerned about is making sure your motives for marriage are pure, and you connect yourself with someone who aligns with your life purpose. Your desire for marriage shouldn't be a self-serving motive because marriage will consist of the unselfish giving of yourself. I know that I'm emphasizing the importance of preparing for marriage, but let's just say you put in the hard work to prepare your heart for marriage and never get married. You have prepared your heart well for interdependence, and you will always accomplish more with others than you can alone. The tools and strategies for doing this internal work will be helpful, regardless if you get married or not.

So, who is the book for? Yes, this is a book for anyone who is single and desires to get married. This information can serve as preventative care for your future marriage. Additionally, this book is for couples who are considering marriage in the future of their relationship, or are currently engaged. And lastly, this book is for married couples. If you feel like you didn't quite do the prep work needed to get ready for marriage, you can prepare now for a new season in your marriage. Things are not too far gone, and the right perspective, information, wisdom, and skills could assist you with creating a brand-new marriage that starts with a brand-new you—conditioning and examining your heart for God's best in marriage, allowing God to heal the places that need his delicate touch and healing balm.

As an overview, the first half of the book focuses on the individual work needed to position your heart in the right place for marriage, and I entitled the first half as "Self-Work." The second half of the book focuses on preparing yourself for marriage with knowledge and skills you can utilize for a successful marriage, and I entitled the second half as "Marriage-Prep Work."

The Bigger Picture of Marriage

We must also look at marriage from a larger worldview than just our personal happiness or individual, self-actualization goals. Marriage is still a good and honorable institution. However, our hearts as a people and generation, overall, have become hardened to marriage. Marriage is so critical and important because it serves as the foundation for families. We also must consider the well-being of children. Research has unequivocally proven that children fare best when they are raised in a stable, married home. In no way am I condemning other family structures, because I believe that all parents want what's best for their children regardless of their marital status. However, it remains true that happily married parents serve as a critical protective factor for their children.

This is a whole new thread to this conversation, but I must go here. In contemporary culture, we've become so focused on ourselves that even marriage is about self. We don't quite have a full understanding of the purpose of marriage, which is to serve your spouse and help your spouse get closer to the version that God always had in mind. The self-serving mentality of marriage and relationships has even invaded one of the most selfless positions of all—being a parent. Many people today believe that having children will be an inconvenience because it will take them away from their personal goals. Our vision has become so shortsighted, and we have lost sight of generativity, legacy building, and so on. Marriage is not about you. Just like everything else in life, it's about your service to the Lord. Marriage is a beautiful vehicle for making an impact on this world and future generations.

What can I promise with this book? What I can promise is that if you put in the hard work of conditioning your heart for marriage, it will profit your life in some way and the generations to come. "All hard work brings a profit" (Prov. 14:23a NIV).

PART ONE

Self-Work

CHAPTER 1

The Power of Preparation

"Preparation is the greatest sign of your faith."
—Dr. Myles Munroe.

"When you get tired, you perform at your level of training/
preparation."
—Joshua Medcalf[1]

"It's better to prepare than repair."
—John Maxwell

YOU WOULD NEVER RUN a marathon without training and preparing for the big day. However, we put more planning and training into our careers, athletics, and education than we do preparing to build a life with someone else. If you are reading this book, you are an exception to this pervasive rule. The truth is that success isn't something you stumble upon; it's something you prepare for, and marriage is no different. People want to hop into marriage with no preparation or internal work and expect to be successful. I'm talking about more than just premarital counseling. There is internal work you need to do on yourself in relation to your heart, emotions and desires before you try to do life with another person. Out of all the areas in our lives, it seems like we have the most wishful thinking for our relationships, and it's an area where many of us isolate from the direction and oversight of the Lord. Failure is almost inevitable when taking this route of naivety.

So, what does it mean to prepare? It means—"to put in proper condition or readiness."[2] Preparation is extremely powerful because it has a way of easing your fears because you've prepped yourself for what's coming next. Prepare also means—to prepare, contrive, devise, imply planning for and making ready for something expected or thought possible. To prepare is to make ready beforehand for some approaching event, need, and the like.

Preparation is a way to apply works to your faith, and faith without works is dead. Faith is such a powerful asset because walking into marriage is a step of faith. I love how the definition of "prepare" indicates planning for something expected or thought possible. Having hope and expecting marriage is key to preparation. In addition, faith is a powerful tool for addressing your fears related to marriage. Preparation is a prerequisite for success, and the success of marriage is too important to leave up to luck or chance. Success occurs when opportunity meets preparation. The reality is that opportunities will present themselves, but you want to be ready. The way you prepare is by addressing the condition of your heart and your mind-set. The wrong mind-set can cause delay or a complete forfeit of the promises of God. You must "be willing and obedient to eat the good of the land" (Isa. 1:19). This willingness comes from the right posture of the heart and mind. For example, when the Israelites first approached the promised land after they were traveling in the wilderness, the negative mind-set of ten spies caused a delay of forty years for their entry into the promised land. This mind-set was due to the condition of their hearts and a lack of faith. Hopelessness can incite behavior that works against the godly desires of your heart, and this is especially true for marriage.

Putting in the Work That Only You Can Complete

The only person you will have complete control over in any relationship is yourself. If you are reading this book prior to entering a courtship or marriage, you are truly engaging in critical personal development that will produce relational dividends for your future marriage. It's so much easier to work out the kinks within yourself before you intimately introduce someone else into your life. Your focus will not be on the other person or on the dynamics of the relationship with that other person. You want to make sure that you can be trusted with your own soul and taking care of your own heart, emotions, and desires before you take on the responsibility and privilege of being a good steward over a marriage and nurturing the heart and soul of another.

You see, the basis of any good and healthy relationship is being able to serve as a secure base for the other individual. You don't want to constantly be the source of anxiety or the heightening of someone's negative emotions. This can pain the heart both figuratively and physically. Therefore, the best test of how you will be able to handle someone else's heart will be how you take care of and address the well-being of your own heart. For instance, if you liken it to the concept of working out, it's like wishing your partner was fit, but you haven't done the work to keep your own body in shape.

Preparation Isn't Equivalent to "Feeling Ready for Marriage"

Have you ever prepared well for a test in school, but knew there was additional time you could have spent studying for the test? Let's just say that you became overly concerned about making sure you were prepared enough for the test, and you pulled an all-nighter only to sleep through the test. You missed your opportunity to perform. You can always spend more time preparing, and even though it is in my heart to help you prepare as much as possible for marriage, I don't want you to fall into the cycle of trying to be perfect before marriage—it's never going to happen. As a matter of fact, you won't ever reach that goal of perfection in marriage. There comes a time when you must perform and utilize what you have trained to do. It's the walking it out that expands your capacity beyond what you could have accomplished through the preparation process alone. There's something you learn from being in the game that practice alone can never teach you.

You may never feel completely ready to make the transition into marriage. Understand that it is a building process. Faith and a willingness to move forward and work things out are important prerequisites. Don't worry about chasing the feeling of being ready for marriage; you may never completely feel ready for marriage. The preparation for marriage is all about conditioning your heart, mind, and spirit for the tasks involved in marriage. Yes, you can always have more preparation, but don't get stuck in the idea of chasing perfection to qualify you for marriage. Many people are stuck in this cycle only to wake up and realize that they missed great opportunities to move forward in this area. It is a good time to stop being reliant on your feelings to guide your decisions in regards to marriage; feelings are flippant and ever-changing. Any step forward requires faith, and marriage is no different. Preparation will change you—just like conditioning prepares your body for a sport. Preparation prepares your heart and mind for the journey of marriage.

The Conditioning Process

Back in high school when I played basketball, we had about two months of conditioning prior to the start of the season. Conditioning didn't even occur on the basketball court—conditioning started on the track and field. Conditioning didn't mean practicing or running drills and plays. No, conditioning was the hard work that was needed to prepare one's body to sustain the rigor of the game. Conditioning was a requirement to try out for the team, and no one was exempt from it. Even for those who were super talented and played on the team before, they still had to participate. All skill levels had to go through conditioning regardless of talent, ability, past performance, or track record. Most players hated conditioning because it tested the limits of their bodies, but in the end, it strengthened their bodies and helped them perform at a higher level during the season. I remember some players throwing up on the side of the track, but they would return day after day and week after week to prepare themselves for the season. During the conditioning process, most players recognized that they would also need to make some changes off the track. They would need to change their diets and sleeping habits.

There is so much richness in the process for conditioning for a sport, and this is also true as it pertains to marriage. There will come a season—a time when the environment, circumstances, and key players are in place for your training to be fruitful. What's important to realize is that there is a period before that season—a time when it's essential that you put in the work on yourself. This is the time for your body, spirit, and mind to be transformed and to be prepared to handle the season well and excel. You don't want the right timing, conditions, circumstances and key players to be in place if you haven't yet done the work on yourself. It won't be fruitful. The time to prepare is before great opportunities present themselves. The way to prepare or condition your heart for the season of marriage is to make your heart fit for marriage. The seeds you plant are the word of God, practical application, time, and trusting the process. Even during physical conditioning for basketball, we had to eat wisely and maintain a healthier diet. The same is true for the conditioning process for marriage—you must be conscious and selective of what you listen to, what you talk about, and what your eyes consume. You can't entertain and feast on negativity toward marriage, then expect your heart to be in the right place for it. Guard your heart and mind from all the negativity on social media, the toxic messages found on regular TV programming, and casual conversations that speak against marriage.

I am a little older and well beyond my high school years of playing basketball, but now I can see how some of my friends missed wonderful dating and marriage opportunities because their hearts weren't in the right place. Good, godly men were interested in them, but their hearts weren't in the right place to receive what was being offered. Now, it's ten to fifteen years later, and the paths that their damaged hearts led them to haven't proven to be fruitful. They are in the same, if not worse, condition than they were ten to fifteen years ago with little to show for their apprehension but wasted time. I know what it's like to have a mind-set that is not fruitful for marriage. I was in graduate school, and I remember speaking against marriage because I thought it wasn't a possibility for me at the time. I told myself that I didn't really want to get married and that marriage could wait—I needed to focus on my career. I was even receiving messages from family members and friends that reinforced this train of thought. What I didn't recognize was that I was speaking from a place of hopelessness and unbelief, and this state can lead to bad behavior or engaging in acts that go against what you truly want in marriage and life. We sometimes feel like we have forever, but this is a lie of the enemy and a surefire way to procrastinate and miss out on opportunities. However, the beauty is that God is a redeemer of time, and I'm still hopeful for people in this situation. My goal is to help you on the front end so that you don't have to look back on your life retrospectively with "what if's" and regrets. Time is moving, and there is a future generation looking to us to get healthy, godly relationships and marriages right. They want to learn from our example. Now is the time to prepare for a healthy marriage not only for ourselves but also for the generations coming after us. We have the power to set on course a legacy of healthy marriages. It starts with us, and it starts right now.

CHAPTER 2

Complete Surrender

Surrender
- *"to yield to the power, control, or possession of another upon compulsion or demand"*
- *"to give up completely or agree to forgo, especially in favor of another"*
- *"to give (oneself) over to something (such as an influence)"*[1]

THERE I WAS, JUST ending an engagement, and I told the Lord that I would not start dating anyone until I consulted him for his approval, first. We did the food tasting, had a date, and I tried on dresses, but it all came to an end after much godly counsel and prayer. I look back on that time, and I see the Lord's faithfulness because the second most important decision after choosing the Lord as your personal Savior is choosing whom you will marry. Even though I thought I was moving forward in good faith, the Lord had to re-route me. I always had a slight catch in my spirit and apprehension about marrying this individual, but I thought certain factors could be covered by grace and love. I felt like our future marriage would be blessed because we had a godly courtship that honored God. We were both virgins (the self-righteous side of me thought we were special because we upheld this standard—this had to be a one-way ticket to a godly marriage and marital bliss). Thank God he showed me and forgave me of this self-righteousness. The truth is that a godly courtship doesn't entitle you to anything, and Jesus's blood covers everyone's past. To be honest, even though I was a virgin before marriage, there were still areas of sexual purity that I struggled with during my single days.

You see, the Lord knows you better than anyone else, and he also knows who is good for you. You can try to do all that is within your power to force things to work, but you want to make sure that your union is something God has ordained because he knows the end from the beginning. You may both be saved and love Jesus but not be a good match for a life partnership. God is concerned about who you partner with in life because this decision can affect your walk with him, the fulfillment of your purpose, and ultimately, your destiny.

To be honest, I wasn't listening to the Lord during my courtship and engagement to my ex. God sent alarms to my spirit during our friendship and courtship, but the Lord gave me the clearest direction when my ex proposed to me. I don't want to seem overly spiritual, but God has a way of getting your attention. As he was proposing to me, I had an open vision of someone else proposing to me. The Lord spoke to my spirit and said, "This will happen to you again very soon and it will feel right." Up to that point, I had never experienced an open vision in my entire life. As my ex was proposing to me, it didn't feel quite right. Something was off, and I was not at peace with moving forward. Yet, I went to try on wedding dresses, and I couldn't make up my mind on a dress. I ordered one dress, and I called the retailer to cancel the order. I think my spirit knew deep down that this wasn't the right thing for me.

Even though we went through with the engagement for months following the proposal, that sense of peace never came.

It all came to a head when several months before the wedding, my ex told me he wanted to postpone the wedding and indicated that he didn't know when a good time would be to get married. I was crushed. This was the same person who told me since we were eighteen—over a period of eleven years, at the time—that God told him I would be his wife. All the plans we made about where we would live, our professional plans, and so on were put to a halt because he indicated that he no longer felt comfortable with those plans and didn't want to get the short end of the stick. I was so devastated. I did the two things that I knew to do—pray and seek godly counsel. I fasted for about a week, and I asked the Lord to give me one hundred percent clarity on whether I should move forward with marrying him. I surrendered my will completely to the Lord. I gave the Lord full authority to determine the outcome of that relationship, and I told him that I would be obedient to his guidance—whether he told me to move forward with the marriage or to discontinue the relationship all together. When I tell you that the Lord gave me clarity and direction, that's exactly what he did. Through specific scriptures that I just so happened to read during that week, sermons, and godly counsel, I knew that I couldn't marry this individual. At the beginning of my fast, I was an emotional wreck. Within a few days, a sense of peace and determinism came over me, and I knew I had to end the engagement altogether. I prayed that the split would be as amicable as possible, and when we met to discuss the future of the relationship, he opened with how he didn't want to put my life on hold. It was a mutual decision to end the relationship. Wow! The Lord truly worked that thing out, and I'm so grateful that I didn't try to force a union that the Lord didn't have in mind for me.

After receiving one hundred percent clarity and guidance from the Lord to end the relationship, I was so content in my relationship with the Lord and being single at the time that I also told the Lord I wanted to take a break from dating. I was at a place of total surrender. I gave my romantic life to the Lord. Now, I don't want you to have to bump your head like I did. I'm all for learning from the trials of others to avert unnecessary pain from your life. I would say the most important step for preparing your heart for marriage would be to surrender your love life to God—all areas of it—and acknowledge and follow his way of doing relationships.

Surprisingly, the Lord had an amazing blessing for me on the other side of surrendering my love life to his will. Within less than a month's time of ending my engagement, Ronnie Bolar, my good friend from college called me out of the blue. When I picked up the phone, he sounded surprised to hear my voice because he thought he was calling his supervisor at the time; her name is Cassandra, as well. He accidently called me because my name was right beside his supervisor's name in his phone. Mind you, we didn't talk on a regular basis since we had been out of college, which was over eight years ago at the time. We were truly platonic friends during college, and we never went out on a date. That accidental call led to a deeper friendship that progressed into marriage in less than two years. I thought it would take years before I would start dating someone again, but God had another plan in mind. I'm a living witness that God is faithful and can be trusted with your love life. My mom told me that my husband was right around the corner after my initial engagement ended, and boy was she right! I couldn't have created a more beautiful love story than the one my husband and I have.

As an encouragement to you and your current situation: In the creation of your love story, God is not limited. I was living in a rural town in Mississippi – where there weren't many eligible bachelors – when my husband called me on accident. He was in Atlanta at the time. I was offered a job in my highly specialized field within weeks of my engagement. Our entire courtship was long distance, and I moved to Atlanta one month after our engagement to live rent-free with my family until the day we married. Our pastor also paid for our honeymoon. God is not limited, and I hope that God will blow your mind when you get an opportunity to live out the love story that he has in mind for your life.

I know surrendering is a hard process, but when you surrender to the Lord you end up gaining more than whatever you gave up. You can either surrender willingly or unwillingly, but the unfortunate part about the latter is the possibility that you will endure much hardship before you reluctantly give your relationship life over to the Lord. We can have the best of intentions and hope that a certain relationship will go well. However, if we don't uphold the Lord's standards or invite him in to guide the course of our relationships, those relationships will be the source of heartache instead of joy. This is due to the nature of our emotions and desires being off-course. We are relational beings created for connection, but the wrong connections can be detrimental to our overall emotional well-being, which can indirectly affect our desires. "Bad company corrupts good character" (1Cor 15:33b NIV).

We can either learn through tribulation or revelation. When we learn through tribulation, we sometimes can hurt others and ourselves in the process. You've probably heard of the popular saying that "hurt people hurt people." Well, that is exactly true. I want you to serve as a healing agent for your own heart and the heart of the person with whom the Lord wants you to share your life.

Giving Your Relationship Life Entirely to the Lord

When you are in the position of surrendering, you recognize and acknowledge openly that your efforts have been unsuccessful. You retreat and seek the help of another person or an entity greater than you. We must reach a place where we recognize that trying to put things together in our own strength (even if our intentions are good) will not be fruitful and is keeping us from the very thing our hearts desire.

You must literally submit your relationship life to the Lord. Give him full permission to connect or disconnect you from people. Remember that opportunity has a way of meeting preparation, and you can't be afraid if God says "no." It would be better to get a "no" from the Lord now rather than investing years into a relationship—or even a marriage—in which you weren't making the right decisions because you didn't seek counsel from God. But let me tell you that those who trust in the Lord will not be ashamed. This is more than true. God can be trusted with your heart. Remember that your heart also includes your desires. God knows your desires, and he can be trusted with them and can bring out the true essence of the desires he placed in your heart for marriage.

Let me also be clear in letting you know that joining yourself in marriage is more than just finding a like-minded, saved individual. You see, God sees your future, and he knows the plans he has for your life. Your vision is limited, but his isn't, and that is why you must trust his guidance and judgment; he sees and knows things that you can't even begin to perceive or comprehend. God is so invested in the purpose he placed inside of you, and he understands the power of partnerships. Therefore, God wants to place you in a life partnership with someone who will assist in bringing out the intentions he has for your life.

After the engagement ended, I was in a place where I told the Lord that I didn't want to date anyone unless I got peace from him to move forward. I got so serious with God, and I told him that I wanted the next person I dated to be my husband. I told him I would not move forward with dating anyone until I got a release and confirmation from him in my spirit that it was okay to proceed. Even after I received peace to move forward with my now husband, there were times during the early days in our relationship when I checked in again...and again. I told the Lord that I was completely comfortable with not progressing with the relationship if it wasn't His will.

You may ask, how do you determine if a relationship is of the Lord? Here are a few indicators:

- You are both committed to upholding the Lord's standards in the relationship. If the person you are considering believes waiting until marriage to have sex is old-fashioned or unreasonable, then you know this isn't someone you should move forward with in a relationship. It will only lead to compromise. Missionary dating oftentimes leads to the missionary position, if you know what I mean.
- You have a sense of peace about the relationship and moving forward.
- You each have a complementary goal to support each other's life purpose.
- You are genuinely interested and compatible with the individual on multiple levels:
  - Spiritually
  - Intellectually
  - Physically

Commit Yourself to Doing Relationships His Way

Not doing relationships God's way will lead to heartache. There is no way of getting around this truth and principle; therefore, I'll repeat it again to emphasize its importance. Not doing relationships God's way will lead to heartache. According to research, couples that cohabit before marriage tend to have lower marital satisfaction and lower marital stability in comparison to couples that don't.[2] This is especially true when the decision to cohabit wasn't coupled with a desire to get married in the future. It's a popular belief of many that it is best to try things out by cohabiting before committing marriage. However, this goes against God's standards, which are put in place to protect us. There is no way of getting around the requirement of upholding God's standards in intimate relationships. Principles are true and work regardless of how you feel about them. I have counseled so many women and men through their relationship issues, and a consistent root cause for the heartache of most of the people I've counseled has been failing to keep God's standards in their relationships. I completely understand the notion that people are imperfect, but you must be committed to doing relationships God's way. When you honor God in your relationships—I promise you—he will honor you in this area.

Also, you want to be as sober as possible when making the important decision of who will serve as your covenant partner in life. Because this person can have such a great impact on your entire life, this person can be used to catapult you forward and closer to your God-given destiny (which is better than what you have envisioned for your life), or this person can be used to stagnate your growth. No one is perfect, but you want to make sure you are partnering with someone who will support your God-given dreams. For example, at Carnegie Mellon, "researchers studied 163 married couples and discovered that people with supportive spouses were more likely to take on potentially rewarding challenges."[3]

Relationships are so powerful—because the people we enter relationships with have a degree of influence over our lives, and you want to make sure that the influence is positive. Oftentimes, many mistakes we have made in life can also be traced back to a connection to the wrong person. Marriage is too important and has such a strong influence over every area of your life; you can't afford to have the wrong influence.

Influence is a wonderful thing, especially when it's in the right direction. That is why you want your mind and heart to be sober when choosing someone with whom to build your life. This person will have a strong degree of influence over your life in ways you may not be aware of at the time, but in retrospect, you will be able to distinguish this clearly. I'm talking about even basic things such as how you dress, how you eat, and even how you see and navigate the world. You want to be with someone who has a sense of "get-up-and-go initiative", especially when it comes to the things of God. You want to be with someone who has a deep personal relationship with the Father because it will get easier to let your relationship with Jesus slide if your closest partner and accountability person is slacking in this area.

Ladies, influence is so powerful, especially when it comes to your husband because he will quite naturally take on a leadership position in your marriage. So, before you get married, you must ask yourself if you are willing to follow this man's leadership. Do you want to go in the direction where he is headed in life? Do you trust this person to parent children with you effectively? Think about the long-term future when considering the person with whom you want to build a lasting legacy.

The longer you continue doing things your way, the harder it will be for you to work with the one God has for you. You see, your heart isn't meant to be broken repeatedly—it has a way of becoming calloused, and you don't want your heart to be in that condition when it comes time for you to be vulnerable with the one God has for you. For example, "Bradford Wilcox, the director of the National Marriage Project at the University of Virginia, pointed to research his organization has sponsored that indicated how having many serious relationships can pose a risk of divorce and lower marital quality. (This can be due to a person having more experience with serious breakups and potentially comparing a current partner unfavorably with past partners and relationships.)"[4]

The Power of Abstinence

Practically speaking, I know that some people don't want to commit to a lifetime of partnership with someone if they believe sex wouldn't be enjoyable with that person. That's the wrong mind-set; your love life with your spouse is something you have a lifetime to grow, develop and learn about one another. Interestingly, research has also shown that living together before marriage—which oftentimes includes sex before marriage—is related to a higher likelihood of divorce.[2] God's standards for sex really do have our best interest in mind, and they serve as a means of protection. The risk of soul ties to the wrong person becomes irrelevant, for the most part, when you haven't engaged in sex with someone you don't marry. This makes parting ways with people so much easier. It makes for a cleaner break. You don't have to see that person for the rest of your life, and you will be OK. You know, it was hard to walk away from my first fiancé, but once I made up in my mind and had peace with the Lord's instruction I felt like I would be totally OK if I never saw him another day in my life. This isn't to be mean but instead illustrates the ease by which I was able to cut the connection with him. In the long-run, having ties with people in your past will only hurt your present and future. You will be distracted by cherished memories of the past with that person. When you get upset with the person God has for you, you may start thinking about people from your past without considering the fact that you broke up with those people for a reason.

You see, sex is so much more than the physical. In comparison, what differentiates sex for humans from sex between animals is that humans don't have sex just to fulfill an urge. Sex can be gratifying and intensified due to the multiple levels we can connect during sex—physically, emotionally, and spiritually.

Let me explain how we get soul ties. Oftentimes, we think of soul ties as some abstract and complex idea, but soul ties are very simple. Your soul consists of your mind, will, and emotions, so a soul tie is when your mind, will, and emotions are tied to another person. Touch connects us with others, and one of the most powerful ways you can physically touch or connect with another person is through sex. OK, now sex is not just a physical act in and of itself. On a biological level, hormones called oxytocin are released during sex, which bond you with the other person. Oxytocin has been called the "love chemical" or "bonding hormone." Sex hardwires your connection to another person. Interestingly, research has shown that more oxytocin is released in women during sex than men—hence, why many women feel more attached after having sex than men do. Oxytocin is the same chemical at work when a mother breastfeeds her child. This chemical helps the child bond to the mother and vice versa. It even helps them both fall asleep. Even though the milk is fulfilling a physical need, it's also fulfilling an emotional and bonding need, and sometimes babies just want to be close to mom and suckle even when they aren't hungry. They may not be physically hungry, but they are eager to bond and feel connected. In your relationships, you don't want to be asleep or unaware when trying to make the important decision about with whom you will spend the rest of your life.

Many have confused love and infatuation—many chemicals are at play in infatuation. Love is a choice, and usually a very selfless act in which you give yourself to another person. The reason why it's so important to avoid sex before marriage is because it truly does cloud your vision. You may think you love someone after sex, but for the most part, you are only chasing a feeling of attachment and infatuation. It can't be love when you haven't consciously decided to give and sacrifice yourself for another person. Choice and free will are so important to God when it comes to love that he even gave us a choice to love and choose him. He's a gentleman, and he doesn't force himself on us.

The concept of love being like a drug is almost correct; infatuation and sex are drugs. However, sex is a very powerful act that can bond us when the time is right, just as the Song of Solomon instructs us to not awaken love before its time. Any time before marriage is not the right timing. However, sex is an important element of marriage because it bonds you to your spouse, and this level of bonding is needed to cleave to your spouse. That's why Paul greatly emphasizes the importance of showing your spouse due benevolence and fulfilling each other's sexual needs. Yes, sex is a need that should be fulfilled only in marriage.

With a soul tie, we connect the feeling of infatuation—or any good feeling from the relationship—to that person, and the stronger the positive feelings, the stronger the tie. It can affect your mind, will, and emotions. You begin to associate positive feelings with that person. Interestingly, things can change so easily; when you start to experience negative feelings with a person and those feelings predominate, it's easy to associate that person with the feeling and want to distance yourself from that person.

Soul ties can cause you to move forward in a relationship for the sake of convenience rather than conscious decision-making. Remember, making a sober choice is an important aspect of choosing a godly spouse. In the case of operating in an unauthorized soul tie with someone who isn't your spouse, you find yourself sliding into decisions that don't work in your best interest. Research also supports this. For example, Stanley, Rhoades, and Markman have created a research model termed the "Slide vs. Decide" model.[5] Their research has found that when couples slide into making major decisions about sex, living together, getting pregnant, and so on, they have lower levels of commitment to the relationship and are more likely to experience problems in the relationship than if they were to make mutual, conscious decisions to move forward in these important areas.

You don't want to invest in something before the market is ready to receive it or before it knows the value of what you have to offer. Making great investments in a relationship before the proper time makes it hard to get out of the relationship because we have a natural desire to see a return on our investment. Some people are in relationships with the wrong people because they invested too much time and energy; the byproduct of giving so much of themselves is that they wouldn't back out even if they could. "Do not arouse or awaken love until it so desires" (Song of Sol. 8:4b NIV). Having proper boundaries in place and upholding God's standards will help you prevent this outcome. Some investments should only be reserved for your life partner and covenant. Regardless of how your spouse may respond to your investment, the Lord will honor the investment you make in your covenant because he honors marriage, and you made a promise to God. You will not be ashamed for waiting on the Lord.

To make it completely clear, it would be best to avoid all types of intimate touching, because you can be intimate or sexual with someone without having sex. You want to avoid the very appearance of evil; if you wouldn't engage in the activity on the front pew at church or at your place of work, you shouldn't do it behind closed doors. This alone will provide clarity in deciphering if this is a good person with whom to enter into a relationship. It is important to remember to not do anything that would grieve the Holy Spirit. Also, when the Lord is writing your love story, you want to make sure you don't flip the script by adding factors or experiences that would take away from the grandeur of what he is trying to create.

In the case of an abusive relationship, it's so easy for outsiders to see the negative effects on the victim and encourage that person to get out of the abusive situation. Oftentimes what we don't recognize is that the person is chasing a feeling of love and connection with the abuser. People become in love with the honeymoon phase during the cycle of abuse, and they are chasing that feeling. Most bad behaviors stem from a desire to chase a certain feel-good feeling or escape negative feelings. Victims of domestic violence can become numb or blind to the abuse and have difficulty removing themselves from the relationship. In some cases, it can even become dangerous to leave. For a relationship that has incorporated sex, both people may become blind to how the relationship is truly hurting them. Each has become tied to the other person through an unauthorized soul tie.

To be clear and straight to the point, sex is the major way in which people–Christians included—fail to uphold God's standards for premarital and dating relationships. Many outright reject this biblical principle. Don't measure your walk with Christ by what other Christians are doing—even if they are your friends. Oftentimes we rationalize our bad behavior by telling lies to ourselves, such as, *well at least I'm not doing so and so like one of my friends*, or *God understands I'm human.* Out of the same mouth and heart we'll say we truly want the Lord to come through for us in our relationships, but we don't come through for him when he entrusts us with an opportunity or tells us to steer clear from the train wreck ahead. Additionally, a lack of hope that things will progress toward marriage is also a factor that leads to bad behavior in relationships. Not doing relationships God's way will complicate your life. Drama, STDs, heartbrokenness, and wasting time are all potential byproducts of doing relationships by the world's standards.

When you really dissect why people who know better still find themselves missing God's mark and standards for relationships, you will find it is because they lack hope. Hopelessness drives bad behavior. "Hope deferred makes the heart sick" (Prov. 13:12a NIV). So, if hopelessness makes your heart sick, that means hopelessness affects the well-being of your emotions and desires.

Let's examine bad or unhealthy habits. People resort to bad habits as a way of escaping emotional pain. They use bad habits as medicine for a sick heart. A state of emotional distress oftentimes serves as a trigger for a bad habit.

That's why faith is so powerful and important when you are conditioning your heart for marriage. Faith and hope are in the sovereignty of the Lord, regardless of the outcome in your relationships. Understand that his will is what is best for your life. God is trustworthy and faithful. We must have so much faith in the good that God has for marriage or our relational well-being that we don't want to do anything that could negatively impact what God has for us. "For I know the thoughts that I think toward you, saith the Lord, thoughts of peace and not of evil, to bring you to an expected end" (Jer. 29:11). Faith in a positive future is so powerful, and research also demonstrates this truth. The Adolescent Health Study (AD Health)[6] found that when adolescents have a strong positive orientation about their future, they are less likely to engage in risk-taking behaviors.

A great deal of the heartache we go through in relationships is self-inflicted. However, we must be very prudent and wise. "For the prudent man foresees evil and hides himself, but the simple pass on and are punished" (Prov. 22:3). It's important that you honor the other person, also. Even if this person doesn't become your spouse, this person will possibly serve as a spouse to someone else, and you don't want to engage in activities that will hurt this person and cause issues for a future marital relationship. I know you would hope someone would do the same for your future spouse.

Date with Godly Intentions

Get beyond frivolous dating. Date with the intent to look for a marital partner. If you know this person is not even close to what you prayed for, don't entertain the desire to be entertained. It will get old, and the joke will eventually be on you. Respect yourself and the other person enough to not waste time. We can't pursue a godly institution with worldly strategies and expect to be successful: Colossians 2:8 (AMP) says, "See to it that no one carries you off as spoil or makes you captive by his so-called philosophy, intellectualism and vain deceit (idle fancies and plain nonsense), following human tradition (men's ideas of the material rather than the spiritual world), just crude notions following the rudimentary and elemental teachings of the universe and disregarding [the teachings of] Christ (the Messiah)."

Let's just say you believe that you are with the person God has for you, but you made mistakes when it comes to upholding God's standards in your relationship. There will be some things you need to cleanse from yourself before you get married; getting married won't sanctify a relationship that isn't honoring God. You want your marriage to have a blessing on it. Granted, we are not perfect, but you need to renounce behaviors and actions you committed with each other before you walk into the marriage covenant. Whether it was sleeping together, living together, or committing other sexual acts, take those to the throne and ask for forgiveness. Follow up that confession with actions that are in alignment with God's standards. The Lord is a forgiving God, and he wants to bless you, but you must apply his principles—they are there to protect and bless the both of you.

Sexual standards exist for the protection of both parties involved. If things don't work out, you don't have to deal with a spiritual tie to that individual. Also, it is easier to walk away if this is not the person God has for you.

There may be people reading this book who believe that they are with the one God has for them; however, they are struggling with sexual purity. I don't care if you are engaged; you still have a responsibility to lay your sexuality at the altar and commit yourself to doing your relationship God's way. Because at the end of the day, you don't want to create an altar for sex in which you sacrifice your spiritual beliefs. If anything, you want to create an altar that glorifies God in which you sacrifice premarital sex. This will be difficult; however, the Holy Spirit will empower you with the ability to live this out. Be extremely practical and err on the side of caution. Put boundaries in place ensuring that you won't be in a position to have sex. If you honor God in this area, he will surely honor you and your relationship. I understand that sexual purity may get harder as you grow older, but you are still God's child. It may seem to get harder because there isn't a sense of hope for truly doing it God's way. That's another reason why it's important—especially when you get older—to date with the intention of getting married. You will know early on if this person is not a good match for marriage. Don't play around with an individual's emotions and time. It will produce a hopeless situation. Hopelessness in a dating relationship is fertile ground for behaving in ways that go against your standards. Move on now.

An essential component of surrendering your love life to the Lord is through the actions that directly follow your verbal confession. You may say you submitted you love life to the Lord, but living out godly relationships will be the evidence proving that you are submitted to the Lord in this area.

Now that we've covered the foundational step of surrendering your love life to the Lord, Chapters 3, 4, and 5 will cover three important aspects of the healing process of the heart as it relates to relationships and marriage. A healthy relationship requires a healthy heart, and if your heart is damaged, there are certain steps you can take to heal your heart: 1) examining your heart (Chapter 3); 2) forgiveness (Chapter 4); and addressing your fears (Chapter 5).

CHAPTER 3

Examine Your Heart

Examine
--to inspect or scrutinize carefully
--to observe, test, or investigate (a person's body or any part of it),
especially, in order to evaluate general health or determine the cause
of illness.[1]

LET'S GET TO THE Heart of the Matter

According to the Bible, the heart is the spiritual part of us where our emotions and desires reside.[2] Just like the human heart is responsible for pumping oxygen-rich blood throughout the body to fuel the organs and every cell and tissue throughout the body, the condition of your heart, spiritually, fuels your perspective and existence on every level—both big and small. That's why the word says to guard your heart above all else, for out of it flows the issues of life. For instance, our emotional well-being—which is a matter of the heart—affects our perspective and the way we view the world. Not only does the condition of our hearts affect our emotions, but it also affects our desires. I would say that the retreat from marriage we are seeing within the millennial generation stems from negative emotions based on personal experience or what we've witnessed others go through in marriage. Therefore, the desire to marry has been negatively affected. Granted, we still highly esteem marriage, but there is a deeper, negative emotional disposition toward marriage that affects our desire and perspective.

So, let's take a closer look at the different components of the heart—your emotions and desires. Emotions are not bad; God gave us our emotions for a reason. They are signals of our unique responses to the environment. We can use these signals as information; the key is to not be ruled and controlled by our emotions. Experiencing emotions means that you are alive; even on a very basic level, babies can express emotions, and they are essential for their survival early in life. A major sign of maturity is the ability to regulate your emotions. By definition, an emotion is "an affective state of consciousness in which joy, sorrow, fear, hate, or the like, is experienced, as distinguished from cognitive and volitional states of consciousness."[3]

A desire is a longing or craving for something that brings satisfaction or enjoyment. Desires can be influenced by many different factors. That's why it's so critical to examine the condition of your heart to ensure you are longing for things in life that are in alignment with what God wants for your life.

Who Sits on the Throne of Your Emotions?

The Bible explains how the heart is the seat for the emotions and desires. A part of preparing your heart for marriage is going through the healing process that is needed for the times when your heart was unguarded and exposed to elements and situations that hurt you at the very core of your existence.

Take heed to Proverbs 4:23 (NIV and KJV, respectively):

- Above all else, guard your heart, for everything you do flows from it.

- Keep thy heart with all diligence; for out of it are the issues of life

To "keep" means:
- *to hold or retain in one's possession—hold as one's own.*
- *to maintain (some action), especially in accordance with specific requirements, a promise, and so on.*
- *to cause to continue in a given position, state, course or action.*
- *to maintain in condition or order, as by care and labor.*
- *to maintain in usable or edible condition, preserve.*
- *in Hebrew, to guard in a good sense (to protect, maintain, obey, and so on.)*[5]

To "guard" means:

- *to keep safe from harm or danger; protect; watch over .*
- *to keep under close watch to prevent escape, misconduct, and so on.*
- *to keep under control or restraint as a matter of caution or prudence.*

No one—other than the Lord—should be seated on the throne of your emotions and desires. This even goes for marriage itself; being single or married cannot sit on the throne of your emotions. You can't give anyone or anything that control. Therefore, your state of joy and contentment should always remain constant and on course due to your relationship with the Lord. This must serve as the well, springboard, and source of love for all other relationships. Understand this truth now before you get married, so that you aren't disillusioned by marriage. Also, this means that your heart cannot be broken beyond repair to the point that it is hardened and unusable unless you give your consent. Even when people do things that hurt you, if they aren't seated on the throne of your emotions and desires, you can always take those situations back to the Lord. He is the only one who should be seated on the throne of your emotions and desires. Your relationship with him should be the security by which you live and experience your life.

You want to preserve yourself and be in the best working condition for your many hats and roles in life. You want to be usable for the Master's use because that is the source of your fulfillment. Your fulfillment will come from making progress on fulfilling the personal call God has on your life. Marriage should be used as an agent to help further the vision, but marriage, in and of itself, will not completely fulfill you. A healthy marriage can add to your joy, but it shouldn't be the primary source of your joy. There is a God-sized hole in your heart that only he can fill. Let your personal relationship with the Lord be the ultimate relationship that fills your cup, so that you will be able to sufficiently pour into the other important relationships in your life.

Desiring Marriage: Guard What You Want for Marriage

It's important to keep in the forefront of your mind what you truly want for your marriage. Hold yourself accountable and responsible for doing the personal work that is in alignment with your vision. The interesting thing about the condition of our hearts is that it can possibly affect our vision or the belief in the possibility to achieve a potential vision. Many people have talked themselves out of believing in marriage or their desire for marriage due to the hurt and pain in their hearts. They believe it may not be a possibility. So, even though deep down they may desire marriage, they speak against it and say that it isn't for them. This is a trick of the enemy to keep you from the pure desires God has placed in your heart.

In other important areas of our lives, it's quite simple to envision the possibilities and become proactive in achieving the vision. However, we oftentimes think that if we are proactive in positioning ourselves for marriage, in some way, we think we are outpacing God. No, faith without works is dead. Ruth positioned herself at the feet of Boaz. Additionally, it's important that you keep that positive vision clear so that temporary negative emotions or less than ideal circumstances don't get in the way of your belief in having a healthy marriage and family. We sometimes become so far removed from our positive hopes and desires for marriage. But consider what it felt like for you as a child and the pure desires you had for family and marriage. Let that level of purity remain present in your current outlook on the possibilities for your marriage.

The reality is that we must know what we are striving for because it's hard to recognize something if you don't have a clear mental image of it. Many people indicate they want a healthy marriage, but they haven't clearly defined what that looks like. Therefore, they base having a good marriage on feelings, and feelings can fluctuate. A clear vision will serve as an anchor for identifying what a healthy marriage consists of, and this clear vision will assist you with creating smart goals for your marriage. It's also important that you speak life into this vision and remain in the habit of speaking life into your positive vision of marriage even after you get married.

You Are Worthy of Love

This stems from addressing fear and unforgiveness within yourself. No matter what you have gone through in the past, you are worthy of having a healthy marriage. Even if you may have hurt people in the past before you knew any better, you are still worthy of love. Even if you made mistakes regarding sexual purity in the past, you are worthy of love. Those experiences don't have to negatively affect your marriage. Allow the Lord to wash you with his blood, and he will keep no record of wrongdoing because that's what true love does.

Additionally, if you are subconsciously trying to prove that you are desirable to others or to a new prospective love interest to show your ex that others want you, you need healing for your heart in the area of self-worth. You are trying to validate yourself through attaching yourself to someone else. You must know that you are worthy regardless if someone is interested in you romantically. Additionally, this mind-set is also an indication that a piece of your heart is still tied to your ex in some way. Part of preparing your heart for marriage is ensuring that your heart is not tied to anyone from your past.

Examining Your Heart

Love is not the icing on the cake of life. It is a basic primary need, like oxygen or water. (Dr. Sue Johnson)[7]

The basic function of the heart is to supply the body with oxygen-rich blood to keep us alive and functioning properly. Loving relationships serve as positive fuel for our heart. Figuratively speaking, love is like oxygen. We are meant to experience it and share it with others. There's an openness needed to take in oxygen, and there is an openness needed to take in love. Search for the areas in your life that may cause you to want to close yourself off from others, or from love in general. Search for those times in life when you felt unloved, and allow the Lord to heal you in those areas. Allow him to show you your immeasurable worth and value.

The preparation involved in marriage is not about achieving perfection, but about conditioning the heart and mind for the journey and process of marriage. Therefore, you must take inventory and be honest with yourself in identifying the current state and condition of your heart. Only you truly know how you are faring emotionally and how your emotions are affecting your desires. Are your desires truly godly desires? Are there some unhealthy or ungodly desires you haven't addressed? If you aren't aware of the potential issues you are dealing with as a single person, you may be unaware of what issues may try to rear their head in your marriage. You must be aware of the strategies or issues that the enemy has used against you in the past, so that you can be proactive in addressing them in the future.

Questions to Ask Yourself When Examining Your Heart

- Do you have an anger issue, financial troubles, control issues, and so on? It's important to identify the root cause of these problems now and reconcile the emotional source of your distress in these areas.
- What are your emotional triggers (sensitive areas that may remind you of strong negative experiences from your past)? When the sensitive areas are touched upon, your reaction may have a great deal of passion or negative emotion.
- It's important to identify the driving emotional factors that may reinforce unhealthy cycles related to your bad habits. It's important that you make headway in overcoming these habits or at least identifying ways that will prevent you from falling into the cycle related to your habit.
- An easy way to identify the hard areas of your heart is to identify the aspects of yourself that you don't quite like or give you discomfort.
- For example, —harshness, distrust, low self-esteem, and so on.

The Process of Conditioning Your Heart

At a very basic and physical level, the heart is a muscle. Therefore, you can condition it. Your heart utilizes blood vessels as the pathways to reach every tissue in your body to supply it with oxygen-rich blood. Your heart also removes carbon dioxide and other waste. However, the elasticity of these pathways is determined by what we consume. These blood vessels can become hardened or softened by what we consume, and we have a choice in that matter. Additionally, as we age, we are more susceptible to the risk for hardened blood vessels due to the accumulation of plaque over the years.

It's our responsibility to condition our hearts and be in the continual process of removing the waste that can choke off our optimal functioning. This is what it means to be diligent and vigilant about keeping and guarding your heart. It's a continual process; there will always be waste agents you must rid yourself of to retain the health and vitality of your heart, emotional well-being, and right, godly desires. The beauty of examining and conditioning your heart is that the Lord supports you in this process and wants you to succeed. He understands the negative implications of a stony heart and how it can ultimately lead to turning you away from the things of God. Therefore, in Ezekiel 36:26 (NLT), he said, "And I will give you a new heart, and I will put a new spirit in you. I will take out your stony, stubborn heart and give you a tender, responsive heart."

Examining your heart is an uncomfortable endeavor because it requires exposing the more vulnerable sides of yourself and getting to the root cause of your hurts and pains. Beyond examining the condition of your heart in general, it's going to be important to examine your heart as it relates to marriage. Is your heart hardened toward marriage? Specific indicators of a hardened heart toward marriage are an indifference toward marriage and a denial of your desire to get married, even though deep in your heart you know you want to get married; jealousy toward others who are getting married; and a desire for others to fail at marriage. Additionally, it will be important to explore your heart toward the opposite sex. Do you have an underlying pain, anger, or resentment toward the opposite sex? These are important questions to ask yourself and address because how can God bless you with something you secretly despise?

The Condition of Your Heart: A Matter of Life and Death

It isn't surprising that the top two leading causes of death in the world are heart disease and stroke. According to the World Health Organization, heart disease and stroke are the leading causes of death, respectively, and they claimed a total of fifteen million lives in 2015.[8] These two diseases have been the world's top two causes of death since 2000.[8]

In a brief review of biology, according to the Mayo Clinic, heart disease "generally refers to conditions that involve narrowed or blocked blood vessels that can lead to a heart attack, chest pain (angina) or stroke. Other heart conditions, such as those that affect your heart's muscle, valves or rhythm, also are considered forms of heart disease."[9]

Sadly, the first sign of heart disease is a heart attack. I believe the same thing happens to us emotionally. We usually aren't aware of our deprived emotional state, and we can oftentimes deny the true condition of our hearts. Our hearts can be deceitful above all things, and desperately wicked—who can know it (Jer. 17:9)? That's why you need God when examining the condition of your heart. When we continue to feed our hearts with unhealthy things, conversations, and belief systems that foster fear, discouragement, and apathy instead of hope, faith, and love, we can make our emotional hearts more susceptible to heart disease. And surprisingly, we wake up one day with a huge indicator that things are not going well for us emotionally. It could be a panic attack, a divorce, or so many other things.

The reason I don't find it surprising that heart disease and stroke are the leading causes of death in the world is because when you mix in the regular stresses of life (work, family, finances) with less than ideal eating and exercise habits, and add emotional stress to the mix, it's a recipe for an unhealthy heart. However, the beautiful thing is that you can guard all aspects of your heart by casting your cares on the Lord for the regular stressors of life, taking proper care of your temple, and guarding your heart (remaining in control of your responses to life and giving God the seat to your emotional well-being and desires).

Unforgiveness, fear, and hopelessness create toxic stress in your life. These factors can harden and stress your heart both physically and emotionally. In looking at the physical effects of unforgiveness and fear, these two factors put the stress response system into overdrive, and as a result, your heart goes into overdrive to calm you down. This stress response is normal and helps us to adapt. However, being in this heightened state of stress for long periods of time can have a damaging effect on your well-being. More simply, a continual state of this hyper-vigilance can cause a host of health problems—physically, emotionally and spiritually. Fear and unforgiveness are conditions of the heart that are not as readily recognizable as other issues of the heart. Let's take a closer look at how added stress—a byproduct of fear and unforgiveness—affects the physical health of your heart.

In my conversation with a cardiologist who practiced medicine for over twenty-five years, he indicated that continuous stress can elevate your blood pressure and increase plaque, regardless of your diet and exercise. To reduce stress in his own life, he made the hard decision to stop practicing cardiology—his love—due to the stress involved. In less than three years he suffered two heart attacks and had open-heart surgery while practicing medicine. He saw and experienced the direct correlation between stress and heart health.

He further explicated his point by showing me his personal blood pressure numbers for a couple of weeks when he was under a considerable amount of stress. He indicated that none of his daily habits had changed; however, he was under a great deal of stress, and his blood pressure was considerably higher during that time. Not only were his blood pressure numbers higher during that time, but his blood glucose levels were also higher. He charts both his blood glucose (as he is also diabetic) and blood pressure numbers every day. Stress has a way of taking a toll on the health of your entire body. There is such a strong connection between our emotional health and physical health; therefore, we can't disregard the importance of taking care of our emotional hearts.

There Will Come a Test to Determine the Condition of Your Heart

For me, my test was no longer entertaining people from my past once I was committed to someone. I made that mistake before and willingly dated someone from my past when I was already with someone else. I was a hot mess during that time. During 2011, I was dating someone, and a boyfriend from my past contacted me. This ex told me that God said I was his wife (yes, this is the same one with whom I later broke off the engagement), a phrase he had said previously in the past. To be truthful, this statement never fully resonated with my spirit. However, he was the only person who told me that, and I believed him. That did not end well. The same test presented itself about two years later in my life.

So, there I was in a courtship with the man I prayed for in 2013 and later married, and a previous boyfriend from a past relationship that didn't have a proper ending contacted me. I didn't recognize it at first, but he was trying to see if we could possibly get back together. Now, he was a great guy, but I told him that it wouldn't be wise for me to be friends with someone from my past. Fast-forward to ten days later, and my now husband proposed to me. I don't believe that would have happened if I had entertained my past. I had to pass that test before being promoted to a new stage in my life.

My hope and desire is that you will consume healthy information that will assist you with the conditioning process of your heart for marriage. Tests and challenges may come your way, but view them as opportunities to utilize lessons learned from your past. There aren't any ultimate mistakes—just lessons learned that can help you move forward with more wisdom in the future. Join in partnership with the Lord to continuously rid your heart and mind of waste that could negatively affect the functioning of your heart so that you can welcome healthy relational experiences that bolster the physical and emotional health of your heart.

CHAPTER 4

Forgiveness

Then Peter came up to Him and said, Lord, how many times may my brother sin against me and I forgive him and let it go? [As many as] up to seven times?

Jesus answered him, I tell you, not up to seven times, but seventy times seven! (Matt. 18:21-22)

MORE THAN ANY OTHER factor, unforgiveness hardens, plagues, and sickens your heart. It is a factor that puts your heart in a bad condition for marriage. There is a boundless nature to forgiveness that we must exercise. Forgive others who hurt you in the past—this means all disappointments related to relationships and marriage, even the negative examples of marriage you may have seen. Forgiveness is key because it's a tool you will need to utilize in marriage. No one is perfect; your spouse will make mistakes, and you will also. Forgiveness is a maintenance tool that will prevent bitterness and resentment from taking root in your marriage, and these two factors can wreak havoc on your bond in marriage.

Before we even get to forgiveness as it relates to previous intimate relationships, it's going to be so important for some to also forgive parents and other family members. For some, that may even mean forgiving people you never met before. This is so important because unresolved issues and unforgiveness in these relationships from your childhood/formative years have a way of creeping into your marital relationship. These childhood issues can even put a false sense of not wanting marriage or children due to past negative experiences. What I've seen in counseling, from friends, and gathered from ample research is that when people have experienced marital breakdown or the lack of marriage between their parents, they are more likely to have an ambivalent attitude and/or fear of getting married and having children. This can be extremely problematic for creating God-designed families. The Lord is so concerned about repopulating the earth with his seed. Our culture has become so focused on themselves that we have forgotten the basic joy of fostering the development of the next generation. Unfortunately, for many, having children has become an inconvenience that may offset their personal goals. The enemy is trying to thwart the purposes of family by stopping the beginning stages of family formation—marriage. If he can attack marriage by creating a retreat from the institution, he recognizes that he can offset the start of the next godly generation. Interestingly, even when people indicate they are afraid of getting married and having a family, they often find themselves slipping into having a family, but not in the way ordained by God. The goal is to be intentional and led by the Lord in family formation, which starts with marriage.

A closely related area is detaching yourself from every partner who God didn't have for you. Sever all soul ties. You even need to detach yourself from the hopes and dreams you had for the future with people who you weren't ordained to be with because you don't want those cherished memories, hopes and desires to invade your mind when building a life with the person God chose for you.

As a reminder, what is a soul tie?

A soul tie occurs when your mind, will, and emotions are strongly attached to another person. Soul ties are not inherently bad, and you are meant to have them with your spouse.

How do you get soul ties?

- vows or verbal confessions;
- certain conversations can create a strong emotional attachment;
- material things that symbolize a connection;
- gifts, rings, jewelry, clothing, and so on;.
- sex; and
- any sexual contact.

How do you sever a soul tie?

- Verbally renounce all behaviors that led to the soul tie and ask the Lord for forgiveness.
- Get rid of all materials, gifts, or any physical things that were given to you by the other person or things that remind you of the other person (gifts, photographs, clothing, jewelry, phone numbers, and so on.)

Forgiveness is paramount because it can change the condition of your heart; furthermore, this is also true for unforgiveness. I'm not talking in abstract terms; I mean forgiveness and unforgiveness have a profound physical effect on the condition of your heart and immune system. For example, research has shown that forgiveness can reduce your risk of heart attack; improve sleep; and reduce blood pressure, depression and anxiety[1]. Dr. Karen Swartz, director of the Mood Disorders Consultation Clinic at Johns Hopkins Hospital, has found that unforgiveness burdens the stress response system and puts your body in a fight-or-flight response, which can negatively affect your heart rate, blood pressure and immune system.[1] These factors, in turn, increase your risk for heart disease, diabetes, and depression, to name a few.

Research has shown there are pathways by which forgiveness affects your physical health through the following mechanisms: heightened spirituality, improvement in social skills, reduction in negative emotions, and reduction in stress.[2] For example, researchers at the University of Tennessee who were testing the impact of forgiveness found that the reduction of negative emotions had the most powerful effect on back pain, headaches, cold symptoms, medication usage, sleep quality and fatigue.[2] A reduction in stress was the second-most powerful predictor of improved health outcomes.[2] Interestingly, it was the condition of the heart (the reduction in negative emotions) that had the most pronounced effect on physical health. The condition of your heart matters!

The word of God established this principle well before people ever started studying it: Let all bitterness, indignation, wrath, passion, rage, bad temperament, resentment (anger and animosity), quarreling (brawling, clamor and contention), and slander (evil-speaking, abusive or blasphemous language) be banished from you with all malice (spite, ill will, or baseness of any kind). Become useful, helpful and kind to one another, tenderhearted (compassionate, understanding, loving-hearted), forgiving one another (readily and freely), as God in Christ forgave you (Eph. 4:31 AMP).

Also, the wisdom of God's word understands the lasting effects of anger on us. Yes, we can be angry, but don't let it fester. When angry, do not sin; do not ever let your wrath, your exasperation, your fury or indignation last until the sun goes down (Eph. 4:26 AMP). The reason why forgiveness is so critical to address before you get married is because it's a heart muscle you will need to continue to exercise after you get married. You'll also need to forgive your spouse and yourself for certain things because the effects of unforgiveness are the same regardless of your marital status.

You want to make sure you are inclined to empathize with your future spouse, and that you develop that lens now with your current relationships. The grace to forgive needs to be embraced now because it won't automatically happen when the stakes get even higher in marriage. Forgiveness isn't something that people deserve—it's a gift you give away that ultimately impacts you more than the person who receives it.

I don't want to just leave you with these facts without giving you practical steps that you can utilize to help you on your forgiveness journey.

1. Choose to forgive. Forgiveness isn't a feeling; it's a choice. Don't wait until you have more positive feelings about the situation before you decide to forgive. The decision to forgive is something you have complete control over, and that's why it's the first step in this process.

2. Ask the Lord to heal your hurt. All the negativity you have experienced due to the incident, cast it upon the Lord and ask him to heal your heart (1 Pet. 5:7). As was illustrated earlier, your very health depends on releasing this negativity and unforgiveness.

3. See the other person's humanity. Have an understanding that no one is perfect and try to consider the other person's perspective by applying empathy.

4. Let go of expectations. Your decision to forgive someone may not result in a change in the individual or the relationship. Part of letting go is accepting the person for who that person is. However, this doesn't mean that you don't put appropriate boundaries in place for this individual.

5. Put forward action. Spend time in prayer with the Lord to allow Him to assist you with this process. Capture some of your feelings in a journal. Engage in healthy coping

strategies, such as talking to a friend, exercising, and so on. If you need professional guidance, seek that support.

The beautiful and empowering aspect of forgiveness is that it's in your control. It's the posture of your heart that you can control. Forgiveness is a tool you can use to keep and guard your heart because it preserves the health and well-being of your heart, emotions and desires. In thinking about preparing yourself for marriage, it's critical that you start from a baseline of encouragement instead of discouragement. You are likely to have more success in an endeavor when your heart is encouraged rather than discouraged. You know that you have forgiven someone when you no longer respond negatively to that person. You no longer have a desire to retaliate, and you are able to see the person outside of the offense.

Another Danger of Unforgiveness

Unforgiveness serves as a seed for altering your identity, and many believe they are justified for their bad behavior. I've had people come to me for therapy and say that they used to be a nice person, but they now don't even recognize themselves. They behave in such negative and maladaptive ways that they never operated in before. These are all indications of bitterness and resentment. These two factors are the result of unforgiveness. Bitterness and resentment change you in the process. You can't be kind and gentle when bitterness and resentment have taken root in your life. Therefore, forgiveness is the tool that preserves the best version of yourself.

I understand that forgiveness isn't always the easiest task, but you don't have to do it alone. Allow the Holy Spirit to reveal the areas of your heart where unforgiveness may reside. Even before we asked for forgiveness, the Lord forgave us. Walk in his example, and he will show you the way.

CHAPTER 5

Addressing Fear

WE MUST CONDITION OURSELVES to believe and hope the best—not a natural tendency for some—especially in our current culture that's ridden with divorce. According to the "Knot Yet" report[1], more people are delaying marriage or forgoing it altogether, and the average age for entering marriage is 26.5 years old for women and 29 years old for men, which is an all-time high. Interestingly, the average age for the first birth for women in the United States is younger (25.7 years) than the age of the first marriage (26.5 years). People are less afraid of having children than of getting married; however, research has unequivocally proven that children born to unmarried parents are more likely to experience their parents' separation/breakup. This instability leads to less optimal outcomes for these children and their primary caregiver (who is more likely to experience financial hardship due to shouldering most of the financial responsibilities for the children.) This isn't the order ordained by the Lord. The cost of the fear of getting married isn't just a retreat from marriage, but ultimately, our children are the ones who are affected the most. The current marriage rate is the lowest it's ever been in decades, and about half of all children in the

United States will experience living without one of their parents at some time during their childhood. This trend is not only problematic during childhood but also adulthood because many children fail to experience the lifelong commitment of their parents and don't have a tangible example of marriage. This can further perpetuate the cycle of fear related to marriage, and ultimately, a retreat from it.

The very essence of love is believing the best and hoping the best. We must understand that ultimately, the Lord loves us, and He wants what's best for us in all areas of life, including our family life.

Fear has a way of paralyzing you, and it may also disguise itself by causing you to deny the very things you are hoping for deep within your heart. Fear comes from a sense that something is unsafe, and there is a lack of security. Ultimately, our security should come from knowing that we have God who truly loves us and has the best intentions for all the areas of our lives. This security and safety should also be with us when we get married. Ultimately, your trust, faith and security should be in the Lord. If we listen to him intently, he will not guide us wrong in our relationships. A lot of the fear people have is truly based on outcomes that are the result of not being led by the Lord. There is safety in the Lord. Also, get wise counsel before getting married because in the multitude of counselors, there is safety.

Fear is the very reason why some people are in their late thirties, forties, and fifties but still haven't gotten married, when deep down in their hearts, they truly want to get married. The over-spiritualization of marriage is really rooted in fear. The passive approach of "I'm just waiting on God" and "I will do nothing during the waiting process" is also rooted in fear. We wouldn't do the same if we say that we believe the Lord is leading us to go to college. We wouldn't graduate from high school and say "Well, I'm waiting on God to go to college" and never take the

SAT/ACT or apply to schools. Well, this is what many of us do when it comes to marriage.

Remember that you are not just married to your spouse, but you are also in covenant with the Lord and your spouse. Ultimately, the Lord can be trusted with your heart. Place your heart and marriage in his hands. He will take care of you and your marriage. Your marriage is a sacred bond between you, your spouse, and the Lord.

Insecure Attachments During Childhood: The Foundation for Fear in Adult Relationships

We all have a basic, primal need for attachment to others. Our very survival at birth depends on the connection and relationship with a primary caregiver. From this relationship, we develop a specific attachment style, with a secure attachment style being the optimal style that is related to having a strong sense of security, sense of self, and ability to freely explore the world without fear. As a basic overview of attachment theory, the degree to which your primary caregiver consistently met your needs during infancy frames your attachment style and self-worth. There are four attachment styles—secure, avoidant, anxious/ambivalent, and disorganized. A secure attachment is developed when the primary caregiver consistently meets the baby's needs—the baby comes to recognize that the caregiver will be there for the baby, and the baby's needs are valid. An avoidant attachment style is developed when the caregiver doesn't meet the needs of the child, and the child has learned to self-soothe. This child recognizes that the caregiver will not meet the child's needs, so the child avoids the caregiver. In the case of an anxious/ambivalent attachment, the caregiver is inconsistent with meeting the needs of the child. Due to this inconsistency, the child's distress is heightened in order to get the attention of the caregiver and get the needs met. This child learns to resort to a heightened emotional response to get the attention of others in order for the needs to be met. This child is unsure if the child's needs are valid or whether they will be met. The case of a disorganized attachment style occurs in situations of abuse, and you are unable to categorize this child's attachment because none of the three attachment styles are evident. This child learns that the caregiver is dangerous and doesn't have a clear understanding of the validity of the needs. This brief overview of attachment styles is important to understand because they also operate in adult relationships. Essentially, your marriage should be a secure base for adult life. It should be a safe haven for you. Your basic needs for love and support should be validated and affirmed in your marriage.

I highlight the importance of attachment because attachment insecurity can serve as a root cause for the fear of getting married. Even if you have a secure attachment style, there can be factors that make you feel insecure in a relationship. Let's just say that you grew up with the example of having a father who provided well for you financially. This financial security may serve as an important need for you in a marriage. This may also fuel a fear related to the likelihood that a future partner would be able to fulfill this need that was grounded in the security provided when you were a child. This is just one simple example, but there could be a host of ways in which your attachment style can impact your emotional disposition toward getting married. Additionally, attachment wounds or traumas can also have a profound effect on your emotional stance toward getting married. In general, we want to avoid pain at all costs. If you grew up in a situation where the people you trusted most let you down in some way, this may frame your perspective on the likelihood of it happening again in your adult romantic relationships.

Steps You Can Take to Address the Fear of Marriage

1. **Identify any fears you may have related to marriage and recognize their root.** Oftentimes, a driving factor for the fear related to marriage may stem from what we've experienced in past relationships. It could also stem from the negative and/or even the positive examples of marriage that have been displayed before us. It's quite apparent how the negative examples of marriage may drive fear—those are the types of marriages we want to avoid. However, what may be less obvious is how positive examples of marriage may cause some to believe that the marital experience is not possible for them. What situations and circumstances may influence this fear? Profess that your marriage will be different and be determined to put in the work needed to have a healthy marriage.

2. **Profess what you want in your marriage.** We can spend so much time discussing what we don't want to experience in marriage that we haven't spoken or given life to what we truly do want in a marriage. Envisioning the best will produce a sense of hope. Expose yourself to marriage; get an understanding of marriage through repeated exposure to healthy marriages. Talk to couples you admire and ask them about what it takes to have a healthy marriage. This will take away the mystery or belief that a healthy marriage is impossible.

3. **Don't give an ear to any negative scripts about marriage.** You want to examine and address your personal script. Have you told yourself that good people don't exist any longer? Have you told yourself that everyone else is getting married, but you won't get married? Have you told yourself that you don't deserve marriage? Have you spoken against marriage? Many people have spoken against the very things they truly desire in life—namely marriage—because they don't believe they will get married or have a healthy, God-centered marriage. Don't

let your mouth set up a life for you that you truly don't want. Death and life are in the power of the tongue (Prov. 18:21a KJV). I know exactly what it's like to feel hopeless and to turn that into a false belief system that aggrandizes what you can do in your own strength instead of trusting God to fulfill the vision and desires of your heart. For example, when I was in graduate school, I lived in a small, rural town, and it seemed like there was no way I would "get found" or progress toward a healthy courtship. I didn't have any prospects. I started to tell myself, *Marriage can wait. I don't really want to get married. I'll focus on my education and career.* You'll start believing a lie if you tell it to yourself repeatedly. The truth is that we are going to marry something in life. You don't want to wake up at sixty-years-old to find that your chosen spouse was never living or breathing but was something that could never give you anything in return.

a. Avoid listening to others who have a negative script related to marriage. When people have had a negative experience, it can cloud their judgment and perspective. A friend of mine was recently engaged, and less than two hours after her engagement, a random stranger told her, "Don't get married. It's terrible. I was married for 30 years and got a divorce and was miserable." Don't allow someone else's loss to color your lenses of the great opportunity the Lord has before you. Let's just say that you want to get an advanced degree, and someone tells you, "Don't go to college. It's too expensive. I failed out of college my junior year." You would simply brush that off. You must do the same for marriage. Sometimes, people haven't put in the work on themselves or their marriage to reap the rewards of a healthy marriage. Don't let someone else's loss determine the outcome of your life.

4. **Commit yourself to putting in the work needed for a healthy marriage.** Educate yourself on what a healthy marriage entails, build up your hope, and tackle your fears head-on with the power of love. Perfect love casts out fear, and love conquers all. Sometimes we are just afraid of the unknown, and education through books and exposure to healthy marriages can help reduce the fear of the unknown.

5. **Recognize and acknowledge that marriage is a desire of your heart.** Of course, you don't want to make an idol out of marriage or use it for a selfish means of self-validation or actualization; however, marriage is honorable. It's the most stable institution to build a family. How can God grant us with the desires of our heart when we dismiss the very things we truly desire? Oftentimes this dismissal is due to hopelessness. During my time in graduate school, I also began to dismiss the importance of marriage. I started to build up an idea in my mind that marriage was something I should postpone, and I should focus on my career and attaining degrees. When I look back at my mind-set during that time, I realize that it was driven by a sense of hopelessness. Additionally, that sense of hopelessness led me into dating situations I would not have considered before if loneliness and hopelessness weren't the predominant drivers of my mind-set during the time.

   a. Our generation believes that we have all the time in the world; consequentially, we have wasted time and missed opportunities. Don't be dismayed, because God is the redeemer of time. However, we do need to have his perspective on the temporal nature of our existence. I don't know how many times I have heard that marriage can wait. Now, I think it is a wonderful idea to focus on developing yourself while you are single, but make sure that your focus doesn't become a selfish, self-centered pursuit. Years will come and go quickly, and there is a time limit on certain opportunities.

6. **You will need help from the Lord with addressing fear and forgiveness.** Forgiveness and addressing fears can be a great undertaking when you try to do them alone or in your own strength. The truth is that there could be some stony places in your heart due to the wear and tear of life, but God can restore and make those areas new. We don't want to walk in the marriage that the Lord has for us and continue to use the old scripts that are wired to the pain of our past.

   a. Now that you've reached this chapter, you've already gone through the process of examining your heart to identify the factors that could potentially harden your heart, such as unforgiveness, resentment, bitterness, low self-esteem, and so on. Now it's time to place those areas on the altar. Let the Lord know that you need His healing in these areas. You aren't expected to heal yourself. Yes, you have some responsibility in the process, but ultimately the Healer does the healing.

CHAPTER 6

Fullness in Christ: Security, Identity, and Purpose

YOUR SECURITY COMES FROM Your Relationship with Christ

At your very core, you want the love of Christ to be the secure base by which you experience life and understand and value yourself. No one can fill the God-sized hole in your heart that is reserved for the Lord. A fullness in the area that only he can fill will serve as the secure base for you to experience other relationships. It's an illegitimate request and desire for you to want your spouse to fill this place reserved for the Lord. Additionally, much of your personal fulfillment will come from walking out the God-ordained purpose the Lord has for your life. You see, you want to serve your marriage from this place of wholeness. You can't look to your spouse to complete you in ways only the Lord can complete you because you don't want to make a "god" out of your spouse or marriage.

Timothy Keller explains it best in how modern individuals have placed their spouses in the place that was reserved for the Lord to build self-worth, personal fulfillment, and identity.[1] Like no other time in history, we are currently putting more expectations on marriage than ever before. Higher expectations—in and of themselves—may not be a bad thing; looking at marriage as more than just a union to secure one's economic standing in society is major progress. However, making someone the sole source of your fulfillment and happiness is an illegitimate request that will oftentimes be met with disappointment. Research is showing that people want to get a sense of their personal fulfillment and self-actualization from their marital partner.[2] When these expectations go unfulfilled, it can result in people feeling highly disappointed and dissatisfied. There is a God-sized hole in our hearts that only he can fill. We want to make sure that we enter and sustain this fullness in God in marriage. This is the route by which we will be able to unselfishly serve as a partner who can assist with encouraging the development of the best version of our spouse and ourselves.

Discovering Your Identity and Value in Christ

Part of your fullness and wholeness in Christ is having a clear sense of your identity in him and seeing yourself the way that the Lord sees you. You know, I don't know how many times I've read the first chapter of Genesis, but something truly stuck out to me when I came across the word "good" when God was reflecting on his creation. So, in Genesis 1, after the Lord made each new creation, the scripture would end by the following statement: "[A]nd God saw that it was good." "Good" seems like such a trivial word, but this word packs so much meaning and value; it is how the Lord sees us. Let me break down the meaning of "good" directly from *Merrian-Webster's Dictionary*,[3] because this is how the Lord sees you and how you must see yourself:

- *Suitable to a purpose; effective; efficient*
- *Producing favorable results; beneficial; salutary*
- *Fertile*
- *Fresh; unspoiled, uncontaminated*
- *Valid, genuine, real*
- *Healthy; strong; vigorous*
- *Financially safe or sound*
- *Honorable; worthy; respectable*
- *Enjoyable; desirable; pleasant; happy*
- *Dependable; reliable; right*
- *Thorough; complete*
- *Excellent of its kind*
- *Adequate; ample; sufficient; satisfying*
- *Morally sound or excellent*
- *Proper; becoming; correct*
- *Able; skilled; expert*

We must have a clear understanding of how the Lord views and values us before entering marriage. Otherwise, you will try to attach your identity and value to your marital status or what significant others think about you. Additionally, it's also easy for us to attach our identity and value to what we do for a living. I know this was especially true for me. When I stopped working in the world of academia as a professor for a season, my self-esteem, self-worth, and happiness plummeted. It was so hard for me during that time because I put so much of my worth and value in my professional accomplishments and positions. I felt lost when I walked away from that world to truly pursue my life's calling, but I'm so thankful for sound teaching and coming to understand that my identity and worth weren't tied to my professional career. God loves me because I'm his daughter. I love to see children and families thrive—that's my identity. God is much more concerned about who you are instead of what you are doing. He is shaping us to reflect his character. Statuses, positions, and careers change, but purpose never changes. Let your identity reside in how God sees you and the purpose He has for your life. "And ye are complete in him, which is the head of all principality and power" (Col. 2:10). Let this sense of wholeness serve as the foundation on which you build a partnership in life.

Your Purpose

God placed you here as an individual with a purpose. You must have a clear understanding of your meaning for life before you are joined with another person. You must understand what makes you unique and your purpose for living. How can you create a life with someone else when you don't know the meaning of your own life? Having this understanding will be important because a significant amount of your personal fulfillment lies in doing what you were purposed to do on earth. Additionally, it's important for your purpose to have compatibility with your spouse's purpose. You are going to have to support your partner's purpose in some way, and it helps when it's something that genuinely interests you.

Your Purpose: Utilizing Singlehood Wisely

Pouring into your purpose is so critical for your time during singlehood. You want to gain some level of proficiency and start to experience the fruit of your labor. For men, this is especially important because you will serve as the leader and visionary for the family; you want to have clarity on where your life is going and where you want to lead your family. As a reminder, true fulfillment comes from fulfilling your individual purpose. This principle is also true for marriage. Your fulfillment will come from fulfilling your purpose. The only thing that will change once you get married is that your purpose could potentially be enhanced or adapted in some way, but the basic root of your purpose will remain the same. The calling of God is without repentance; God doesn't change his mind about your calling/purpose in life. Marriage has the potential to enhance your life in certain ways, but fulfillment will come from fulfilling your purpose in life.

You must use your time wisely while you are single. It's important to make considerable progress in your individual purpose. This is especially true for women due to the adaptations that are needed to be a helpmeet. When your skillset is well-developed, you serve as an even greater asset in marriage.

Additionally, be honest with yourself regarding your desire to get married. Is marriage something you truly desire? Do you believe God has called you to be married, or do you believe God has called you to a life of being single? If you believe that God has not called you to marriage, it's very important that you live your life accordingly. Why indulge in dating and courtship when you don't believe that God has called you to marriage? If you have a desire to date and court, you may want to reconsider your stance on being single for the rest of your life. You need to move with conviction, focus and intentionality. If you truly feel like God has called you to be single, he will give you contentment for singlehood. However, it may be dangerous to yourself and others to participate in activities leading to marriage when you very well know that you aren't called to marriage. Don't get yourself and others confused and/or hurt by your desire to play around with the concept when you know you will not move toward the end goal of marriage. This isn't to say that you can't have friends of the opposite sex if you are called to be single, but also remember that it takes a special person to live a lifestyle of singlehood for that person's entire life.

Ultimately, you are a gift, and you want to become well-acquainted with yourself before you move into a lifetime partnership. Knowing who you are gives you a keen understanding of the type of person who would be a good partner for you. Having a sense of wholeness before marriage is critical, and you find that wholeness in Christ.

CHAPTER 7

Addressing Selfishness

SELFISHNESS IS THE SULFURIC acid to any relationship—especially marriage. Marriage requires selflessness and sacrifice on so many levels. An important ingredient for a healthy marriage is empathy, and selfishness blinds us to the experiences of others. You know, people don't purposefully fall into the habit of being selfish; most of us know this characteristic isn't ideal. What we may not recognize is that there is a specific precursor to selfishness that serves as the unrecognized root to selfishness—hurt, pain and disappointment.

So, what is selfishness exactly?

According to *Merriam-Webster*,[1] "selfish" means:

- *"being concerned excessively or exclusively with oneself: seeking or concentrating on one's own advantage, pleasure, or well-being without regard for others"* and

- *"arising from concern with one's own welfare or advantage in disregard of others; a selfish act"*

Selfishness can have a sneaky way of surfacing. As mentioned earlier, many people are not purposefully trying to be selfish. Hurt, pain, and disappointment all have a powerful way of making you become entrenched in your own experience, which is a precursor for selfishness. Selfishness can cause you to become deceived by your own warped perspective on your circumstances. I see it all the time with couples in my office who are gridlocked in conflict and/or discontentment. I also see it in myself when I've been hurt or offended by something my husband has done. Having a heart that is readily postured to forgive helps you to consider the other person's perspective and the possible hurt that person is experiencing. However, pain causes you to want to protect yourself at all costs, and getting in the habit of allowing the Lord to heal your heart is a continual process that doesn't end during singleness. You need it even more in marriage, and the healing process is coupled with the process of forgiveness. Selfishness is also harmful because it's a concentrated focus on your situation, and it can indirectly serve as a breeding ground for depression because you are so focused on yourself. It's hard to be depressed when you are thinking more about the needs of others rather than focusing only on yourself. Focusing on yourself and your feelings is a natural response to feeling slighted or wronged in a relationship. However, you don't want your focus to remain on yourself. Conflict is inherent in a close relationship, but you want to ensure that your focus doesn't become all about you and your needs. Taking your partner's perspective into consideration can be the exact remedy you need to cool off the tension of an intense conflict. You can exercise this ability now without being in an intimate relationship. You can practice with family members and friends.

The seeking of excitement and self-pleasure is also how many affairs get started. The fantasy world of pleasure and a relationship that doesn't include the day-to-day responsibilities of living with another person (budgeting, household chores, child care) can give a person a distorted view; outside relationships appear more satisfying because they only include the pleasurable aspects of a relationship. I see it all the time in therapy.

Conditioning your heart to have a well-rounded understanding that a loving relationship isn't only about your own personal fulfillment/pleasure is key for having a healthy relationship—especially a healthy marriage. A desire to serve others is what is needed for a healthy relationship. Philippians 2:5 says, "Let this mind be in you which was also in Christ Jesus." This passage was speaking of his servant's heart that was concerned about the well-being and interests of others. For example, Philippians 2:4 (AMP) gives us a clear understanding: "Let each of you esteem and look upon and be concerned for not merely his own interest, but also each for the interests of others." So many people find themselves unhappy and miserable because they have believed the philosophy of modern culture that promotes seeking your own happiness regardless of the cost to others. The "do what makes you happy" idea is the very thing that is making so many people unhappy. True happiness comes from serving and giving, but when you are only trying to serve yourself, you will inevitably be unhappy.

Hurt: The Pathway to Selfishness and a Bad Attitude

OK, I have a question. Have you ever met a stank person? No, I'm not talking about a physical odor, but I'm talking about a stinky attitude. Well, the root to a nasty, stinky attitude is self-protection from hurt. People who have been hurt before want to ensure that it doesn't happen again; however, some of their strategies can be maladaptive. So not only can hurt lead to selfishness, but selfishness can also lead to the hurting of others as a means of self-protection—individuals who have been hurt so badly that they don't realize that their self-protective strategies are hurting others and themselves. It can produce a brashness, bitterness, and overall stinky attitude that can be very difficult for others to tolerate. This is how the people who oftentimes need love the most are the ones who are the hardest to love. It is due to their self-protective strategies, which ultimately have a root in hurt, that have led to selfishness.

A lot of bad decisions in relationships stem from putting yourself first and protecting yourself at all costs. This is the direct opposite of love—because love isn't self-seeking. At the heart of the matter, love gives; therefore, selfishness at its core conflicts with a true expression of love. One caveat, however, is that you want to make sure you aren't making a martyr of yourself and neglecting self-care. This also doesn't apply to situations of abuse.

Is Your Motive for Marriage Selfish?

Examine your motive for marriage. If you are going in with a self-centered desire for marriage, you will become disillusioned quickly. Your motive must be bigger than you and your spouse, for that matter. The community should feel the impact of your marriage.

It's going to be important that you condition your heart and shift your focus now from what you want to get out of marriage to what you want to *give* in marriage. Your fullness needs to come from getting your needs met ultimately in your relationship with the Lord and recognizing that no one can take his place or make you feel complete or secure. There are many benefits to marriage, and I think it's nice that these appeal to us. I just don't want you to lose sight of the bigger picture so that you don't become disillusioned by marriage. It's in the giving of yourself that you find joy; think about the times when you have volunteered for a good cause. You didn't serve or volunteer to make yourself feel good, but you fulfilled a need, and indirectly, it made you feel good. Many times, we may not feel like doing good deeds or volunteering, but you always make a situation better when you do, and more than likely, you will feel uplifted in and after the process. The same is true for marriage.

So, my advice is to lean out of situations that may tempt you to be selfish and lean into opportunities to be selfless in all areas of your life. Developing the habit of selflessness now will condition your heart to be strong in this area when you are married in the future.

PART 2

Marriage-Prep Work

I WOULD LIKE TO preface this part of the book by indicating that the preparation for marriage is not synonymous with dating. You can have a lot of experience with dating and not necessarily be well-prepared for marriage, especially if you are dating according to the standards of the world. Additionally, if you don't feel like you are in a season for marriage and need to work on personal areas, dating can be unprofitable and potentially hurtful to yourself and the other person. I'm not a fan of frivolous dating. If you know that marriage is not close in your future and the Lord is dealing with you in your singleness, commit to only being friends with the opposite sex. That means treating opposite sex friends the same way that you would treat your same-sex friends. Friendship is the best foundation for a relationship. Yes, I'm a strong believer of "he who finds a wife, finds a good thing and obtains favor from the Lord" (Prov. 18.22). Therefore, it's very important for men to be courageous and initiators when they feel like the Lord is leading them toward marriage. However, as a woman, that doesn't mean you should just sit at home and wait for your husband to knock on your door. You position yourself as a wife by becoming proficient with your gifts and serving in areas where your gifts are needed now. When the season is right for moving toward marriage, don't be afraid of dating. Create godly boundaries, and you both will be OK, even if the relationship doesn't end in marriage. My only concern is that many people have delayed marriage due to fear, and they could have progressed toward it if they were more proactive. You don't have to wait for all things to be perfect in yourself or your situation before you move in the direction of marriage. Remember, the Lord wants you to succeed in this area, and he will let you know if you are ready to progress toward marriage.

CHAPTER 8

Understanding God's Intent for Marriage

GOD VIEWS MARRIAGE AS being something more significant than a contractual agreement; God sees marriage as a covenant. Biblically, a covenant always involves God, man, a sacrifice, and a promise. "Covenant" in Hebrew means *"in the sense of cutting; a compact (because it is made by passing between pieces of flesh), confederacy, confederate (ally, to band together; a person who helps someone do something), covenant, league (an association of persons or groups united by common interests or goals; a group of sports teams that regularly play one another)."*[1] Whenever a covenant was made, an animal was cut in half, which symbolized how if the covenant were broken, the parties would be as the animal—broken and severed in half. There was a sacrifice made; and the promise was deemed worthy of the sacrifice. So, a covenant means you are on the same league or team. In the natural sense, "covenant" means: *"a usually formal, solemn, binding agreement; 2) a written agreement or promise usually under seal between two or more parties especially for the performance of some action."* (*Merriam-Webster*) Classically, covenants are between nations or other powerful groups (such as in 1 Sam. 11:1 and Josh. 9:6,15). At the international level, they usually involve an alliance between two unequal parties—the stronger one pledging protection and help to the weaker in return for some form of vassal status.[3] Ultimately, your covenant also involves the Lord, and he is the more powerful entity in your covenant who protects the marriage.

Marriage will involve sacrifice, and the way it was designed was such that you don't leave marriage until death do you part. Leaving the marriage covenant before this time will lead to two broken individuals—something or some part will die. Therefore, it's so important to make a sober, God-informed decision before making such an important commitment to God, your spouse, your future/current children, and the greater community. Sacrifice is also coupled with serving your marriage and spouse. The unexpected result of your service is great joy, fulfillment and the positive impact it will make on your marriage.

God's Purpose for Marriage

- Genesis 1:27 (KJV): "So God created man in his own image, in the image of God created he him; male and female created he them."
- Genesis 1:28 (KJV): "And God blessed them, and God said unto them, be fruitful, and multiply, and replenish the earth, and subdue it: and have dominion over the fish of the sea, and over the fowl of the air, and over every living thing that moveth upon the earth."
  - Fruitful: *yielding or producing fruit; abundantly productive; bring results*
  - Multiply: *to increase greatly in number or amount*[5]
  - Subdue: *to conquer and bring into subjection; to bring under control, especially by an exertion of the will*[6]

God utilizes marriage as a vehicle to help us get closer to the version of ourselves he always had in mind. Marriage should help you to become more like the Lord. God is love, and marriage gives us the ripe opportunity to share his love with the one closest to us—our spouse. I'm talking about the unconditional, agape form of love that is highlighted in 1 Corinthians 13. It includes kindness, patience, serving each other, and keeping no record of wrong. This love is a choice that must be chosen daily in marriage. This process doesn't always feel good, but it's good for you. Times may come when you want to be impatient and unkind, but you need to choose kindness and patience instead.

Mark 10: 6-9 (AMP): "But from the beginning of creation God made them male and female. For this reason, a man shall leave [behind] his father and his mother and be joined to his wife and cleave closely to her permanently. And the two shall become one flesh, so that they are no longer two, but one flesh. What therefore God has united (joined together), let not man separate or divide."

One of the most significant roles of marriage is how it serves as a protective vehicle for the replication of God's seed (people) in the earth. God is so concerned about continuing his legacy within the earth, and he uses marriage to do that. Each person is a unique expression of God with a kingdom assignment to bring the will of God to the earth. God's work can't stop, and he utilizes people throughout the generations to achieve His will. Just as Matthew 6:10 says "Thy kingdom come. Thy will be done in earth, as it is in heaven." Having children is how the will of God is achieved on earth on a continual basis. So, how does marriage assist in this process? Marriage is the joining of two individuals as one, and sex joins us as one with our spouse. On a biological level, conception occurs when one cell (the sperm) from the man joins with one cell from the woman (egg), and those two separate cells becomes one cell that goes on to multiply into more than a trillion cells to create a brand-new human being.

This is fruitfulness at its best! The miracle of life. The truth is that when you have sex, God sees the joining of two flesh. This is the very definition of marriage. God sees marriage when sex occurs. That's why sex outside of marriage is unauthorized, because you are essentially demonstrating the act of marriage without being married.

There is a complementary nature to your union; you bring something different to the marriage from what your spouse brings. However, there is such a powerful synergy that occurs when you bring yourselves together. He made men different from women; however, we are both created in the image of God.

Marriage involves a sacrifice and a promise. We have focused so long on the sacrifices and work involved that we have taken our eyes off the reward and promises of marriage.

"Hope deferred makes the heart sick"(Prov. 13:12)

"For all the promises of God in him are yea, and in him Amen, unto the glory of God by us" (2 Cor. 1:20)

There must be a balanced approach in our focus. Focusing on the promises of marriage serves as motivation for the work. The sacrifices don't seem as hard when you know the purpose of your hard work. God puts a blessing on marriage. Research has shown that happily married individuals live longer (this is especially true for men), make more money across their lifetimes, are healthier, and provide stable home environments for their children, on average. Marriage truly does matter; it matters for our personal health and well-being, the well-being of our children, the well-being of our communities, and ultimately, it matters to God.

The Role of Attachment in Marriage

A very important task that needs to be accomplished early in marriage and strengthened over time is a strong attachment and sense of security with your spouse. The "leaving and cleaving" instruction from the Lord refers to the need to develop a new sense of attachment and security with your spouse instead of your family of origin. This means an emotional, physical, spiritual, financial attachment and security. It is your job to do as much as you can to reinforce and strengthen these dimensions of attachment and security in your marriage early on in the commitment. I've seen in therapy how some individuals haven't truly developed a secure sense of attachment with their spouse. That could make it difficult to create boundaries for your family of origin because you may have a stronger sense of allegiance with them instead of your spouse. This is not the proper order.

Building a sense of attachment is the reason why sex is so significant and confined to marriage; you need a powerful mechanism and jolt that will help you attach yourself to someone who was initially outside of your family. Sex is so powerful because it connects you with your spouse on all dimensions—physically, spiritually, and emotionally. You need sex to create that attachment and sustain it over time.

Sex is a bonding process on so many levels, and you can't detach two things that are bonded together without compromising the individual pieces. As a reminder, oxytocin—a bonding chemical/hormone—is released during sex, which builds a bond and attachment to the other person. That's why it's so important to refrain from sexual activity prior to marriage. Many people believe that since they are no longer physically connected to a person sexually, the bond they once had has been totally broken with that person. That's why you must seek the Lord to remove the residue of the emotional and spiritual bond that was made with that person through sex prior to marriage, even if you go on the marry that individual. Sex outside of marriage creates an unauthorized bond that is faulty in nature because it wasn't created in the right environment with the blessing of the Lord. You bound yourself without a promise, lifetime agreement, or covenant. You don't have any sense of obligation or duty to the person if you aren't married, and that's never the context that the Lord intended for an act that connects you on such a strong level. He knows the security that's needed when a strong attachment bond occurs. Marriage protects the binding force of sex, and sex reinforces the connection and bond of marriage. It's a positive feedback loop. However, the positive feedback loop can never occur outside of marriage; oftentimes, the reverse is true. Before marriage, sex compromises the relationship and breeds a sense of insecurity rather than security. Additionally, sex is the powerful mechanism by which life is brought into the world, and God wants that life to be supported by the security of a marriage—the sense of duty, obligation, and covenant—which, in turn, provides the security and unity needed for the offspring of sex, children.

Understanding Your Role: What Are You Preparing Yourself For?

It's quite important that you have a good understanding of what you are preparing for when it comes to marriage, and what you are preparing for in respect to the role you will fulfill in marriage. Just like any job, you want to know what the expectations are so you can have clarity on what you need to do and how to manage your job responsibilities. Some of these responsibilities you will navigate with your spouse, but there are some clear responsibilities outlined by the Bible that will be brought up in this section.

Just like in sports, you must understand the purpose and role of the position you play. This will help the other key players on the team better step into their roles. Regardless of your insight into the game, you must focus on being the best version of yourself in the role you were designed for, and this will enable others to perform better in their roles.

Roles—especially gender roles—have been in flux for some time now. There are so many demands on both roles. Roles and expectations for marriage go well beyond gender roles. Currently, we have more expectations than we have ever had on marriage, and those extend to needs for companionship, partnership in finances, recreational fun, co-parenting, and other important aspects of building a family. Even though there may be some general role expectations for marriage, each marriage will be different. You can create an agreement and decide what is best for your marriage. Trends do indicate that wives/mothers take on most of the responsibilities of the upkeep of the household, and they tend to have a "second shift" after the work day ends. The second shift involves taking care of the household and child care responsibilities after working potentially outside of the home. Also, fatherhood literature has acknowledged that paternal roles are more highly negotiated than maternal roles, with negotiation occurring between the fathers themselves, their partners, and the ever-changing social prescriptions for fatherhood.[7] Times are changing when it comes to the functioning of the family; the methods which used to work even just forty years ago have become obsolete today. We must consider the unique context in which we find ourselves building a life with our partner and apply the wisdom of God's word. Marital roles are different from parental roles. It's important that you figure out what would work best for your marriage and family. Play to your strengths and allow each person to take a primary role in the area of that person's strengths.

Wife
"She looks well to the ways of her household and does not eat the bread of idleness" (Prov. 31:27).

One day, I had an epiphany that my husband needs some help—major help. I realized this help wouldn't require seeking a professional counselor or spending a dime. No, my husband doesn't possess any fatal flaws or defective personality traits. As a matter of fact, he is the most encouraging, appreciative, ambitious and loving man I know. I came to the realization that my husband needs *my* help, support, love and encouragement more than anyone else's. This lightbulb went off when he was in the throes of preparing to launch his own business; without his prompting, I recognized that he would need my help in a very practical, hands-on manner. I also realized that I have unique attributes and talents that would help him in the areas where he would need the most assistance. The hardest part of the realization was understanding the action that would be required of me—namely, making changes in my own life to fulfill this important role. I had been so accustomed to doing my own thing that adjusting my life in major ways to support and help my husband seemed like a sacrifice that was too big for me. I'd spent my entire life specializing in making my own dreams and aspirations come true, and I needed to make an important shift during that time—early on—in our marriage.

I had to do some critical soul-searching to figure out God's wisdom on my role as a wife, and how his insight should guide me in providing the help and support my husband needs. Slowly but surely, my heart softened. Eventually, I was able to fully embrace the idea of providing the help my husband needs—regardless of the changes required of me. I started to delight myself in supporting his dreams in major ways, and he did the same for my dreams. The first step of this journey was clearly defining what it means to be a wife and using God's wisdom on the topic. Then "helpmeet" stood out to me. Now, the English version of helpmeet doesn't quite give justice to the depth and significance of being a wife. The Hebrew version of helpmeet is *ezer* (strength/power/rescue) *kenegdo* (alongside/counterpart), which better illustrates the beauty of being an equal partner with your husband and a source of strength and encouragement.[2] For example, *ezer* was referenced in the Bible during the times when people desperately needed the Lord's help and strength to come through for them.[8] Being committed to providing this type of help for my husband has been a process—albeit a very rewarding process. I have adopted his dreams as my own and vice versa. Additionally, assisting him with his dreams and goals has indirectly poured into my goals and dreams. Never have I been more on track for fulfilling the call on my life. I discovered that supporting his dreams didn't mean I had to sacrifice my own; if anything, my dreams have been enhanced. At the end of the day, this process has led to creating something much bigger than ourselves—a family mission that involves the both of us. For all the newlyweds out there, be encouraged; the changes that are needed to adjust to marriage may seem foreign in the beginning, but they will prove to be rewarding in the end. The help and encouragement needed in marriage may be practical, spiritual or mental, and they have a way of being reciprocal in nature. For all the wives out there, just how your husband needs your help in a desperate way, you'll need his help too! Make your dreams come true together.

You know, no one explicitly explained to me the role of a wife according to the Bible, and I didn't have a clear understanding of that role until I was already married for three years. You see, the wife is the manager of the home—the CEO. God's word indicates that the virtuous wife is the is a productive overseer of her home. "She looks well to the ways of her household and does not eat the bread of idleness" (Prov. 31:27). Wow! I didn't quite know that the role of a wife held so much significance and power. The wife has a powerful role in driving and promoting the well-being and success of the home. Also, I wish I had known that earlier so that I could have more readily stepped into that role at the start of my marriage rather than stumbling across this principle later in marriage. Let me tell you, I'm not naturally inclined to be an efficient organizer or manager, and this is something I constantly work on in our marriage. I saw the effects of disorganization on my well-being, and I knew I needed to make a change. My typical, disorganized way of functioning was somewhat working in the initial days of our marriage because it primarily affected me, but then we had a baby. I recognized that there must be a shift in how I manage our home and myself. As a manager, your ability to manage cannot be ruled by your emotions. You must have clarity and fulfill your role regardless of how you feel. Being a wife is a great responsibility just like anything rewarding in life, but there is a joy and reward that comes from taking care of our responsibilities. I really love the sermon in which Andy Stanley pointed out how someone must make up for or pay for irresponsibility. Failing to take care of your responsibilities has a ripple effect and affects those in your immediate and distant environment.

In specific relation to a wife's relationship with her husband, the wife's role is to support, encourage, honor, respect, and submit to her husband. I know the last term has almost become a byword to many people, but submission is an honorable act that brings blessings into your marriage. If you feel a lot of negative emotions toward the idea of submission, this is a sign of a deeper heart issue. Reflect on the source of this negativity and address it now by utilizing the steps discussed in Part 1. Especially consider the steps for forgiveness. Was it a dogmatic doctrine that promoted a misuse of the husband's leadership role? Do you have some father wounds from your childhood? Do you have experience with someone abusing the husband's leadership role? Allow the Lord to show you the source so that it won't negatively affect the dynamics of your marriage.

Essentially, the wife undergirds the mission of the marriage. To "submit" means "to yield oneself to the power or authority of another; to defer to another's judgment, opinion, decision, etc."[9] Ultimately, your faith and trust as a wife are in the Lord. You trust that the position he has given you will not put you in a bad situation. In situations where you defer to your husband, you are ultimately yielding to the Lord because a godly husband will seek guidance and wisdom from the Lord for his leadership and decision-making in the home. Submission is for the wife and husband, for Ephesians 5:21 instructs the following: "Submit yourselves one to another in the fear of God." Submission is a way for both the husband and wife to reverence and honor God. Therefore, influence goes both ways, and a caring husband will consider your thoughts, feelings, and ideas, and accept your influence, as well. However, there are clear instructions for a wife to submit to her husband: "Wives, submit yourselves unto your own husbands, as unto the Lord" (Eph. 5:22). Submission is ultimately a service unto the Lord. When God instructs us to do something, he always has our best interest in mind. Yielding is a great sign of faith, and it doesn't mean that you are a doormat. Yes, you have influence and authority of your own, and you are willing to lovingly yield your power to your husband. It lightens your load and gives him the opportunity to carry the weight of the relationship, which he is empowered to do by the Lord. Think about what would happen in traffic if people didn't yield to the person who has the right of way. There would be collisions, accidents, and possible death. The power of those two cars would collide. Your trust must be in the Lord that he is leading your husband in the right direction to avoid collisions and accidents and to promote the optimal well-being of your family. Even if he gets it wrong, the Lord can make it right and no problem lasts forever. I recommend reading Ephesians 5:21-33, and allow the Holy Spirit to guide you in this area.

For many husbands, honor and respect are the ways they receive love. It's not just the affection and physicality of love that matters to a husband. Honor and respect oftentimes carry more weight for men than affection. This instruction from Ephesians

5:33b in the AMP version sums it up nicely: "[A]nd let the wife see that she respects and reverences her husband [that she notices him, regards him, honors him, prefers him, venerates, and esteems him; and that she defers to him, praises him, and loves and admires him exceedingly]."

A lot of times, I hear some single women say what they aren't going to do in marriage, but how can you be given the gift of marriage if you refuse to take on the responsibilities of marriage? Every gift comes with a cost, and the cost is usually what makes it so valuable. We wouldn't enroll in school to say that we would never study for class. The focus on what you *won't* do in a marriage stems from pain and fear; that's why those two factors were addressed in the beginning of the book. At the end of the day, you aren't just marrying your husband, but also God will be the center of your marriage. He can be trusted with your heart and you giving your all—you aren't just giving it to your husband, but you are doing a great service unto the Lord and your family.

Husband
"Husbands, love your wives, even as Christ also loved the church, and gave himself for it" (Eph. 5: 25).

For the husband, your role is the visionary and servant-leader for the family. One of the best examples of being a good husband is from Jesus Christ. He was a servant leader who was willing to sacrifice it all. He gave his life. Husbands must be on point with their relationship with Christ to gain godly insight and wisdom on the direction he wants to take the family. When you are married to a godly woman, she is going to desperately need and expect for you to have a strong relationship with the Father. This will also support her faith and agreement with your decision-making and leadership. In learning from the example of Christ, Jesus spent intimate time with the Father so that he could fulfill his mission and get direction. An important thing to know while you are a single man is your purpose and clarity on the mission God has for you to fulfill on earth because it's impossible to lead when you don't know where you are going as an individual. Additionally, you want to find a wife who is suitable for the purpose and mission of your life.

The reality is that as partners, you have so much influence over one another, especially in the role of the leader and visionary of the family. This isn't a bull-headed type of leadership, but this is a servant-type of leadership in which you are willing to sacrifice the pleasures of your own life for your wife and family. It's ultimately a display of your love for yourself and your family. "So ought men to love their wives as their own bodies. He that loveth his wife loveth himself" (Eph. 5:28).

In consideration of Jesus' example, he also fed the church both naturally and spiritually. Your intimate time with the Lord will also provide spiritual sustenance for you to share with your wife. And practically, your wife and family will also need your physical provision of resources—financial, emotional, and so on. I'm not saying that to be a good husband, you must be the primary breadwinner or make more money than your wife—however, you must be a provider. This is a very basic level of giving and leadership that will assist your wife and children with feeling secure. As mentioned before, an important developmental task that must be achieved early on in marriage is leaving the security of your family of origin and cleaving to your spouse. A strong sense of emotional and financial security assists with this process, and the husband drives the development of this culture.

Lastly, Christ beautified the church, which is another layer of provision and serving as a righteous example for us to emulate. "Husbands, love your wives, even as Christ also loved the church, and gave himself for it. That he might sanctify and cleanse it with the washing of water by the Word. That he might present it to himself a glorious church, not having spot, or wrinkle, or any such thing; but that it should be holy and without blemish" (Eph. 5:25-27).

The next chapter is going to be so amazing for men reading this book, and it will also provide insight for women. I'm so excited about this next chapter because my husband wrote it. There's nothing like men speaking and imparting to other men's lives. I know you will be blessed by the information he shares. He and I talk about these topics all the time, and I'm so happy that some of the nuggets he shares with me will also be shared with you.

CHAPTER 9

Man-to-Man

OK GUYS—THIS IS THE man-to-man chapter. It's going to be short and to the point, just the way we like it! As a man, you must ask yourself if you really want to get married, and if you understand what marriage really means. Consider the examples of marriage you've seen. Were they positive, or negative? It may be hard to replicate something you haven't seen. For a man, marriage is going to require education, patience, and consistency (being intentional). Let's explore these three topics. Education is first. As stated before, it can be nearly impossible to replicate something you've never seen or experienced. Some of us have never seen or experienced what a great marriage looks like. Since this is the case, reading this book is a tremendous first step into educating yourself on marriage. Another avenue I would suggest is seeking out a mentor couple. Find a man who is in a committed marriage and ask him to mentor you. This could be a pastor, a family friend or a business partner. Look for a couple that is modeling the type of marriage you would like to have.

"For ye have need of patience, that, after ye have done the will of God, ye might receive the promise" (Heb. 10:36 KJV).

How many of us think we have the capacity to be patient? Not many, I would guess. The reason why is simple; as men, we are naturally inclined to be problem solvers. We don't want to spend any extra time on any one issue. In a marriage, this will prove to be almost impossible to continue. Every aspect of your marriage is going to require patience on your part. From waiting on your wife to get ready to go (ANYWHERE), to getting your children dressed and fed for school. Patience is a virtue you must develop. You will gain it through time and circumstances, both good and bad. Hang in there!

With anything in life worth having, being intentional and consistent is key. Women have an amazing ability to completely forget what we have done for them lately. So, what does this mean? You must be consistent. Now this may sound like a difficult task, but let's examine the other areas in your life where you have been consistent. Remember your consistent workouts? Remember your golf outings and extra shifts at work? We can be consistent when we want to; in marriage, the consistency requires us to consistently give of ourselves—our time, our feelings and our thoughts. These are three areas we could care less about sharing, but they are exactly what our wives need. So be consistent in the areas she cares about, and she will be singing your praises!

I said it was going to be short, right?

Here are a few more bullet points to consider:

- As men, we are the initiators. We must adopt a godly perspective on marriage; it's an asset—not a liability. When you are serious about getting married, initiate and follow through. Let God lead you, and pray with your perspective spouse.
- The responsibility for leadership in this area rests on us as men. Preparing for marriage isn't just a task for women.

The condition of the man's heart will affect the entire marital system.

- Before you get married, figure out what it is that you should be doing with your life as a man, because once you start that process, it will attract a woman who is complementary to your vision and purpose. Your future wife is going to expect you to know what you are doing. You need to be moving in a direction. A woman is looking for leadership, direction, and security.

- There are women out here—good women—who want to be married. Ask the Lord for wisdom, guidance, and discernment when you are looking. It's important to guard your heart by not getting too deeply involved too soon.

- Get rid of the fear of commitment and fear that marriage won't work.

- As a man, you must understand your role. Your role as a husband will evolve over time. In the beginning, you will only be your wife's partner. As time goes on, more roles may arise, such as father, business owner, and grandparent. With you knowing your role, you must understand that it is to be the stability and security of the family. When things go haywire, your wife and your children will be looking to you for answers.

- Most importantly, remember one of your basic needs as a man is recreation. Have fun during this process. The wife and life of your dreams await!

CHAPTER 10

Important Considerations for Choosing a Marital Partner

The Importance of Being Led by God

ONCE YOU HAVE ADDRESSED and conditioned your heart for marriage, you have now positioned yourself to receive good favor from the Lord. However, you want to be led by the Lord's proper timing and wisdom. Marriage will have a profound effect on your walk with Christ and being equally yoked is critical. Who you partner with has the capacity to mature or stagnate your walk in Christ. You are responsible for the ultimate result; however, your marital partner will have a significant influence on how your marriage shapes you as a person, and especially as a Christian. There is so much wisdom to gain from the story of Abraham sending his servant Eliezer to seek among his people a wife for Isaac. Abraham had a keen understanding of how Isaac marrying a Canaanite woman could lead him into apostasy and idolatry. Therefore, he sent Eliezer back to his hometown of Mesopotamia, a four-hundred-fifty-mile journey, to secure a wife for Isaac. Abraham was concerned about Isaac maintaining his faith, and that is why he made Eliezer make a solemn pledge with him. He understood the importance of marrying someone with congruent beliefs and faith.

There are so many salient characteristics that stand out from this story. I would like to highlight the major ones that stood out to me as considerations for what one should look for in a husband or a wife. For a full understanding of this passage, I would recommend reading the entire twenty-fourth chapter of Genesis.

Wisdom to Gain from Eliezer's Example

Unselfishness. Eliezer wasn't thinking about himself or his specific needs when he was sent on assignment to find a spouse for Isaac. Before Isaac was born, Eliezer was originally in line to inherit Abraham's household. However, he unselfishly sought to please Abraham by finding a wife for Isaac. Additionally, after he found a suitable mate, Rebekah, he had a desire to give her gifts and bless her and her family. Unselfishness is a staple characteristic of a good husband because unselfishness serves as a prerequisite to servant leadership. Ladies, when considering if a potential mate is from the Lord, consider his willingness to serve, bless, and give to you. Is he only out to meet his own personal needs, or is he focused primarily on blessing you? Now, I'm not talking about this new concept of how many people are looking for sponsors to support their lifestyle or believe that a man must be a baller or have attained his ultimate position of financial prosperity to be a suitable match. But, how does he share and give what he has? Are his motives for pursuing you pure and unselfish? Is he willing to give of his time and resources—granted, in the dating/courting season, this giving won't be to the same degree as it will be during marriage. However, do his *actions* point to the potential of him being an unselfish leader and unselfish provider?

Faith. Eliezer had faith that the Lord would make his assignment successful. He prayed about the right woman and he was specific in his requests of the Lord. He was in search for more than a pretty face. That wasn't even on his list. He was in search of godly characteristics, such as kindness and her willingness to serve—his prayer that she would provide water for himself and his camels. Additionally, his prayer had the right intentions; he prayed about her display of character. He also had an opportunity to watch her character when she was unaware of his intentions, which also indicates that this incident was more than likely a true display of her character. Even though he didn't pray for superficial characteristics such as beauty, he was blessed to see that Rebekah was beautiful, a virgin, unmarried, and modest.

As the leader of the home, it is imperative that the husband has a strong sense of faith in Christ for the well-being and success of his family. To be led in the right direction, faith is a requirement.

We as believers must also understand that marriage is a walk of faith. The Lord will guide you to the right person when the timing is right. It will be confirmed in your spirit by a sense of peace. Additionally, when you get that release of peace, understand that the enemy may try to make you second-guess God. Just realize, even for good things and what you know God has led you to, the enemy sees it all as a threat and will try to sow seeds of doubt. You must feed your faith during your courtship process.

Understood His Purpose. A man of God will have a keen sense of purpose and know how critical it will be for him to find someone who will serve as a complementary counterpart to his vision and purpose. Having a keen sense of purpose requires spending intimate time with the Lord to discover your identity and develop your calling. Ladies, you want to make sure that he understands who he is in God and has made some significant progress in the direction of his calling. He can't lead you anywhere if he doesn't first know where he is going. Eliezer knew exactly why he was sent on the journey, and he understood the importance of fulfilling his assignment. He was not distracted, and he didn't get weary by the distance he had to travel. He spent time with Abraham to get the proper instructions for his journey.

Moved with a Sense of Urgency. Eliezer didn't play around with time to enjoy the comfort of Rebekah's father's house. He said, "I will not eat until I have told my errand" (Gen. 24:33). In the morning the next day he said, "Send me away to my master" (Gen. 24:54). They asked if she could stay ten days, but he wanted to get back quickly to Abraham. Eliezer had a strong conviction and focus. As a woman, when you are dating, you must ask yourself important questions. Has he shown an indication that he wants to move the relationship forward, or is he only enjoying the conveniences of having a girlfriend? Does he have a strong conviction and focus about how he will conduct himself in a courtship situation? Does he have godly standards for how he will conduct himself in the relationship? These are all indications that he is marriage-minded and doesn't want to take advantage of you. When a man has done the internal work and the timing and conditions are right, he doesn't want to play around and waste time when it comes to finding a wife. He moves with a sense of urgency. It's not a sense of rushing, but a sense of redeeming lost time and a sense of understanding that all opportunities don't last forever—they have an expiration date on them. Additionally, a man of God doesn't want to waste his time or anyone else's, for that matter.

Wisdom to Gain from Rebekah's Example

Not only is there great wisdom to gather from Eliezer, but there is also so much wisdom to gain from Rebekah. The first characteristic she displayed was like Eliezer's, which was an unselfish, servant's heart.

Selfless Servant's Heart. Rebekah went above and beyond what was typical courtesy of providing water for a man; she provided water for his camels also. Eliezer found her working and serving. She was busy being faithful with the tasks placed in her hands. What's amazing is that she was found being faithful, and her character was being observed without her knowledge; therefore, it was a display of character that could be trusted. I believe that it is helpful to watch someone from afar without that person's knowledge of your observance or interest. This way, you can trust what you see on display. Oftentimes, in dating situations, people bring their best representation of themselves to the table. However, we are more of our authentic selves when we don't know we are being watched. That's true integrity.

Willingness. Rebekah had a willingness to follow Eliezer back to Canann. "And they called Rebekah and said to her, will you go with this man? And she said, I will go" (Gen. 24:58 AMP). She had a confident acceptance of Eliezer's request. This is so significant. When a man has made his intentions to marry you clear, as a woman, it is critical that you have a desire/willingness to accept his influence and follow his leadership. Just think about it in the professional sense. We all answer to someone in business and there is a proper chain of authority. It's hard to follow the leadership of someone you don't respect or don't believe has the capacity to lead well.

Roles are continuing to be negotiated, but both men and women must adapt to the new requirements of marriage that differ from singlehood. Especially for women, we are going to have to adapt. Adaptability is not only a trait that is helpful for marriage, but having the capacity to adapt to new situations and circumstances also promotes your mental health. It's not about how you used to do things or how you lived your life prior to marriage. You are creating a new life with your husband, and you need God's skillful wisdom. I love how Proverbs 24:3 (AMP) indicates that "through skillful and godly wisdom is a house (a life, a home, a family) built, and by understanding it is established [on a sound and good foundation]." Your marriage is so much bigger than personal happiness. It's important to get beyond the selfish, individualistic worldview of marriage that only focuses on personal fulfillment. Now, that doesn't mean that marriage is drudgery; you have the capacity to experience much joy and happiness in your marriage. However, the marriage itself will not be the total source of your joy and happiness. It will be an outlet of service, and in the service, you'll find fulfillment. As a reminder, never put anyone on the throne of your emotions—that includes marriage. We're all familiar with the saying that marriage is meant to make you holy—or more like God. Marriage makes you more like God because it is used as a vehicle for you to display his unconditional love, sharpen you, and assist you with fulfilling a work in the Earth that he ordained. Essentially, marriage is about building, and the Lord placed you two together because you have essential and complementary resources and skills that are needed to *build*. You are going to need God's wisdom to build what he always had in mind for you two. It doesn't stop there because marriage is also utilized to create an environment and family culture that is conducive for the healthy growth and development of the next generation.

Refreshing and Fulfilling a Critical Need. A good attitude is refreshing, and it is a powerful asset in marriage. This is critical for both parties, but especially for the wife. We as women have been socialized to better detect the emotional climate of relationships. I know this is a general statement, but at the aggregate level, it is true. Women oftentimes serve as the emotional thermostat for the relationship. We have the capacity to set the emotional tone of the marriage. And as the CEO and manager of the home, this is an important task. I learned from the book, *The Energy Bus* by Jon Gordon,[1] that your heart has an electromagnetic field. The energy of your heart's electromagnetic field can be detected up to five to ten feet away. Also, the power of the heart's electromagnetic field is five thousand times more powerful than the brain. This piece of research referenced in the *Energy Bus* showed me the science behind how people can sense how you are feeling. This makes so much sense, and people are better able to detect how you feel rather than what you are thinking. Think about it. How many times have you been asked if you are OK emotionally? The person asking you this question knows that something is wrong. You know this perceptibility doesn't just work with negative emotions, but people can also sense your positive feelings and these positive feelings are contagious.

So, just remember that as the wife of the home, you are the manager of the home, and you are driving the emotional climate of the home. No one wants to work for an angry, fault-finding, negative manager. The same is true for your marriage and family. It's hard to cooperate with a spouse who is constantly negative and has a bad attitude. Challenges will occur, and life will happen, but your attitude is something you have an opportunity to choose each day. Based on that choice, your situation will become harder or easier due to the perspective your attitude gives to the situation.

It's also refreshing when someone provides a critical need in an area where you are lacking. Rebekah provided water for Eliezer and his camels after their long journey—a five-hundred-mile journey. A man's journey will have some hardships. A wife provides a critical component that a husband is lacking. That's why we are complementary in nature. Until the end of time, a man is missing his rib until he finds his wife.

Intrigued/Attracted to Issac. Also, the first time that she saw him, she found him in prayer and meditation (Gen. 24: 63-65). Sometimes, the best way to get to know someone is when that person is unaware that you are watching and examining that person's lifestyle. This is when you are more able to see the authentic self. This can be achieved by getting to know someone in a group setting before you walk into a dating/courtship relationship. The individual is less likely to present the representative or best self when the person doesn't know you are watching. We must take finding a marital partner very seriously and understand the profound impact it can have on our relationship with Christ. Now ultimately, your walk with Christ is something you are accountable for, and your spouse can't necessarily make you have a close or distant relationship with the Lord. However, your spouse can be an accountability partner, major influencer, and a source of motivation. I love the way Keller explains how your spouse is used as an instrument to bring you closer to the image God has in mind of you.[2]

Wisdom to Gain from Rebekah's Family

Rebekah's family was pleased to give her away to Isaac. Her family also acknowledged that the whole incident was from the Lord. (Gen. 24:50-51). Her family supported the marriage. Additionally, Rebekah was from Abraham's fathers' house—she was Isaac's first cousin. This signifies the importance of marrying a believer (someone connected to God and part of the royal priesthood/family).

When you come from a godly, God-fearing family, it will be important to have their blessing. Even if your family isn't in the position to provide godly counsel, your spiritual parents, pastors, and leaders should provide some type of approval of your marriage. If God ordains your future marital partner, you shouldn't be ashamed or hesitant about presenting your spouse to your family and spiritual leaders.

Things to Remember:

1. God is on our side when it comes to putting together people for a godly marriage. He will prosper your way (Gen. 24:40).
2. There must be a willingness and desire for the marriage on both sides. The solemn oath of Eliezer to find a wife for Isaac would have been nullified if Rebekah or her family were unwilling to let her marry Isaac.
3. The Lord will clearly reveal if the person who sparks your interest is a suitable marital partner (Gen. 24:14). It will all be based on that person's character. Don't be afraid to seek the Lord's insight and direction. You would much rather find out whether a person is suitable for marriage and ordained by God prior to taking the steps toward getting married, rather than finding out this information retrospectively.

Factors to Consider Prior to Marriage

An Intimate Relationship with the Lord

First and foremost, is this person a believer? Does this person have an intimate relationship with the Lord that bears fruit? You want someone who is in tune with God's love and his virtues because this will give your future spouse the proper foundation for loving you. The reality is that you don't want to be tied to someone in the most intimate way possible—through marriage—if the person doesn't have a relationship with the lover of your soul This is Bible 101—don't be unequally yoked with unbelievers. A yoke is used to tie two working animals together. There will be tension and a desire to move in different directions if you miss it in this important area—being believers and having a similar maturity in Christ. An unequally yoked connection will hold you back; a nice person could be bad company for you. Bad company corrupts good manners. You can't marry someone's potential to be a believer. This will be an area that frustrates you in the future.

An important prerequisite for being equally yoked will be having both individuals committed to doing relationships God's way. You can also be equally yoked in ways that may not be spiritual in nature—meaning that you have similar core values. For example, are you both interested in health and exercise? Do you both value family relationships and want to have children? On the spiritual front, you want to make sure that you feel comfortable being your authentic spiritual self with a potential marital partner. This means that you would feel completely comfortable worshipping God, praying, and giving when you are around this person. I recall dating someone who seemed to clearly fit the bill when it came to a future husband (he was a minister and loved the Lord). However, I didn't quite feel comfortable being my authentic spiritual self around him. We had conflicting views on factors related to worship and prayer. I almost felt censored and restrained in a way, and I knew that I wouldn't want to live the rest of my spiritual life and relationship with the Lord in this way.

Family Background

You will interact with your spouse's family, especially if you plan on having children. This person's parents will become your children's grandparents. You want to consider how this person was raised and how your future spouse's relationship with his parents has shaped him. What's running through their generational bloodline? Granted, the blood of Jesus covers all, but you want to be conscientious of these factors. Did they experience distant relationships during childhood? How was this person's relationship with the father, in particular? It's important to have keen insight on these factors. Also, the reality is that no one comes from a perfect family, and understanding someone's family background will also give you compassion for that person's experience. This compassion will be needed, and you could potentially help foster healing from childhood wounds. Also, you want to make sure you understand what you are getting yourself into.

Don't Get Blindsided by the Superficial

What could make for a good boyfriend could possibly not make for a good husband. For example, a fun-loving person who has a hard time with accepting responsibility will not make a good spouse or parent. What are the deeper qualities and characteristics that would be ideal for a spouse? The word of God can be your reference point—the fruit of the Spirit and the true meaning of love (I Cor. 13: 4-8). A person can be as saved as that person wants to be and still have an anger problem. Don't overlook these factors; they become amplified in marriage. As we discussed earlier, premature intimacy can make you very susceptible to turning a blind eye to the important character flaws of an individual. As a caveat, no one will be perfect—not even you! However, there are red flags that you must pay attention to and consider. Many factors could cloud your discernment and vision, such as sexual activity, physical/monetary assets (you can build together), only paying attention to the person's physical appearance, and the fictional storyline that you created in your mind about how the relationship will turn out.

Repeated exposure and experience with someone will reveal character. It's these experiences that you want to view as soberly as possible. Pray to the Lord to reveal to you if it would be wise to proceed before you get deeply involved with someone. Even if the relationship doesn't end in marriage, you have exercised yourself in a godly manner and can leave without heartache. At the end of the day, no one belongs to you until you are married, and you want to treat all the people you date in such a way that that person's spouse won't have to clean up the negative aftermath of that person's time with you. Don't you want the same when it comes to your own spouse?

The Importance of Friendship

It's so important to have a solid friendship with your spouse. Friendship should serve as the foundation of your attachment to one another. What do friends do? They spend time together; they share important aspects of their lives together; and they have fun with one another. There are going to be some mandatory business aspects of marriage—finances, taking care of children, and household chores—that must be managed. You don't want your marriage to get lost in the business aspects. You want to make sure that you foster your friendship by doing things together that you both enjoy. It saddens me when I see couples who never spend time together. When I see them out, they are always alone. Marriage isn't meant to be this way. No, you aren't obligated to spend every waking moment with each other; however, it is important to spend the quality time together doing things you enjoy that foster a sense of fondness and appreciation of one another. Research has shown that doing new activities together releases dopamine, which is the neurochemical that makes you feel pleasure.

I believe it is helpful to start off with friendship before moving into the romantic realm too soon. This gives you an opportunity to observe a person without that person being aware of it. There are people out there in committed relationships with people they don't truly like; they jumped into the commitment or became physical before they understood the person's character and compatibility. There are some amazingly nice people out there who are saved and love the Lord; however, that doesn't mean that they would be a good match for you. If you can't be friends with someone, then you can't be that person's spouse.

Consider the Long-Term

Consider if the person is someone with whom you can go through all seasons of life. Granted, people do change over time; however, do you want to change with this person? Does this person possess the characteristics that would make a good parent? Is this person forgiving? How does this person handle conflict? These are all important questions you want to ask yourself, and you want to have a long-term perspective on what would be important for the future.

Define the Roles of Husband and Wife for Yourself

Explore and identify your personal definition of what it means to be a husband and a wife. It's important that you have a clear understanding of what these roles mean to you because you will subconsciously measure yourself, your future spouse, and your marriage by them. It's also important that your personal definition of these roles is influenced by what the word of God says about these roles. It's important to speak to a prospective mate about your understanding and expectations for these roles prior to getting marriage so that you are not blindsided by unmet expectations. I liken it to an annual review for a job where you know the criteria used to rate you when the job starts. When you have a clear understanding of the expectations and goals of a position, you are more likely to achieve them and excel. Also, remember you will only be in pursuit of pleasing the Lord and your spouse when it comes to the responsibilities of your role. Don't worry about what friends, parents, or family members may say. Are God and your spouse pleased? That is what truly matters.

I can remember having an underlying sense of discontentment during our first year of marriage. It stemmed from me not fulfilling the personal expectations I had for myself as it related to marriage. I was almost numb to this feeling because I was so focused on my job and trying to fulfill work expectations. Let me tell you this, regardless of how noble you may feel your work is, nothing is nobler than serving your own family well. That's your first ministry. I felt like my lifestyle and the way I was spending my time were not congruent with my values for marriage or my expectations for myself in the role of being a wife. I was so inundated with work that I wasn't truly present when I was at home, and I knew I didn't want this to turn into a habit and norm for our marriage. It was so bad that I would talk in my sleep about work, of all things. I had a wake-up call when we experienced a miscarriage. I remember being in the bathroom stall miscarrying our first baby at work. I got up, cleaned myself off, and went right back into the conference room to help lead a meeting. I didn't fully process what happened at the time, but I was able to look back and see that I was pouring so much into my job at the expense of my family life. You know, I waited a while to get married, and it had always been my dream to have a healthy marriage and family. However, how I was walking out my life at the time wasn't truly congruent with my values for marriage or my expectations of myself as a wife. My miscarriage caused me to look at my life differently and acknowledge the stress I was under from being consumed by work. I didn't want that for my life. I knew there was something more, and I knew I needed to make an adjustment. So, with strength I didn't know I possessed, I walked away from that job. I walked away from the prestige of the field. I walked away from the money. I walked away from it all. My health and stress levels, my husband, and my family were too important to be left with the leftovers of me. What helped me make a change in relation to work was my value system related to marriage and the role of being a wife. Having a clear understanding of what you value in marriage and your specific role in marriage will serve as an anchor and guide for your choices and behaviors in marriage, especially the hard choices.

It will also be important for you to consider how you will prioritize the new role of being a spouse, and how you will continue to prioritize this role for the rest of your life as your seasons in life may change—for example, having children or taking care of elderly parents. Getting your mind-set into the role of being a wife or a husband is an important preparation strategy that will enable you to walk out the responsibilities of marriage without them being foreign to you.

The following are some practical tips:

- Complete a study of passages of Scripture that discuss marriage and the roles of marriage. Make sure that this study also incorporates a focus on love and the fruit of the spirit. Ephesians 5:21-33, Proverbs 31:10-31, 1 Corinthians 13: 4-7, and Galatians 5: 22-23 are good places to start.
- Make sure that you have high—but realistic—expectations for these roles.
- Consider factors that may have influenced your personal views on the role of being a husband and wife—and on marriage in general.
- Try to reconcile or discard factors that aren't truly helpful and don't measure up to the word of God.

Have a Basic Understanding of How You Handle Conflict

Conflict is inevitable in life, and it also presents itself in marriage. It's a misconception to believe that conflict indicates that something is wrong with your marriage. Conflict—in and of itself—is not a bad thing. It's all about how you manage conflict. I meet so many conflict-avoidant people in therapy, and they believe that they are making the situation better by not addressing the concerns they have. However, what happens is that the unaddressed conflict stockpiles, and they eventually blow up or behave in a way they regret later. Dr. John Gottman has done research with couples where he examines the heart rate and stress response systems of couples during an argument, and what he found was that the person who shuts down and doesn't discuss the conflict at hand has a more distressed stress response system and higher heart rate.[4] So physiologically, the person who avoids the conflict is more distressed internally than the person who tries to address it.

There are healthy ways to address conflict, which include the following steps:

1. Become aware of the heightened emotion you are experiencing.
2. Take a break and cool down.
3. Identify the underlying softer emotion that may have driven you to more intense emotion.
4. Consider your partner's perspective.
5. Use "I" statements ("I felt a certain way when this specific thing happened") to express your underlying softer emotion. The beauty and reasoning behind this is that expressing softer emotions is more likely to engender connection rather than defensiveness. For example, when someone tells you that person is sad about a situation, you are more inclined to listen and have compassion. However, when someone expresses irate feelings, you are more likely to try to defend yourself or flee the conversation.
   a. As you are letting the person know how you feel, it's important to start with a soft startup. Acknowledge something good the person has done or identify positive intentions before you discuss what offended you.
   b. Only focus on one situation; you don't want to pull up the entire kitchen sink.
   c. State the facts—what happened, when it happened, and how it made you feel?

6. Let the person know what you would like to see instead of what was experienced.
7. End on a positive note (for example, acknowledge the person's good intentions and progress).

So, before you get married, it's important to understand how you and your potential partner handle conflict. This way, you will be able to troubleshoot for the future, and you can reel yourself in when you see yourself getting stuck in your typical cycle. You'll need a clear understanding of how you manage conflict. Be able to identify when you need to take a break and find some space. Are you a pursuer or distancer when it comes to conflict? Be aware of how your style may affect those around you.

Rid Yourself of the Idea That Marriage Will be a Cakewalk Because You Are Saved

Don't be disillusioned in thinking that since you completed your courtship and engagement God's way, marriage will be a cakewalk. God still requires so much from us. Just like we were stretched in personal areas during the courtship period, marriage will require the same or even more stretching in areas related to personal and relational development. Don't be discouraged by this process. As Keller emphasizes, "Marriage is used to bring you closer to your glorious self in Christ Jesus."[2]

By the time you get married, or after you've done substantial work on preparing your heart for marriage, you won't have arrived. There will always be areas of growth in your life. There will also be areas of growth in your life related to the healing process of your heart, and in some ways, your spouse will help you in those areas, and the Lord will help you in the other areas. Always remember that you will need the Lord to get through marriage. You will always need to depend on him for everything. Be encouraged because you and your spouse are not alone; the

Lord is also with you and he is just as invested in making sure that your marriage is a success.

Lastly, remember that getting married is an act of faith; it takes faith and the Lord to take that step into marriage. Trust that God is your ultimate caregiver, and he has given you the tools or access to tools that will help you have a successful marriage. The choice is yours.

CHAPTER 11

What Happens After Marriage?

THIS SECTION OF THE book is helpful for you now in your preparation and conditioning of your heart for marriage, but this section may resonate with you more after marriage. I encourage you to reread this chapter after marriage as a means of positive reinforcement and encouragement. Here are a few truths you must come to terms with before you get married.

The uncontrollable variables

Variables will present themselves in your marriage. I don't know when it will happen, but it will happen. It could be difficulty getting pregnant, the death of a loved one, the loss of a home, infidelity, sickness, the loss of a job, or financial troubles. This event/blow/circumstance will not be any fault of your own, and sometimes, your spouse may even cause it. If your spouse potentially caused it, remember that your spouse, more than likely, didn't have ill intentions toward you when the infraction occurred. Most likely, your spouse is now willing to do whatever it takes to make things right. It's going to be a journey; give each other patience and forgiveness. Additionally, when you think you may be over it, continuous reminders will be placed in your head that will try to make you react in anger and cause a wedge between you and your spouse. During those times, cry out to the Lord. He is still rooting for you. "Don't faint in the day of adversity. If you faint in the day of adversity, your strength is small" (Prov. 24: 10). This uncontrollable variable is indirectly being used to build your marriage—not tear it down. You will be able to share lessons learned with other people. It's important to have an agreement and plan before unforeseen circumstances happen. You have two choices when an uncontrollable variable happens in your marriage: You can allow it to cause a wedge of distance between you and your spouse, or you can grow closer to your spouse and the Lord to overcome the issue.

The reality is that you may experience distance between you and your spouse when this uncontrollable variable shows up initially, and the task will be to transition from this place of distance where you feel like you are alone on an island to working together to come out of the situation. Isolation breeds emotions and feelings that are not good for your marriage or you. What will assist you in making the transition to cleaving to your spouse and the Lord will be remembering your anchor and the bigger picture. Rough patches tend to smooth over. For example, longitudinal research has shown that when couples experience lower levels of marital satisfaction, after time has passed, they tend to experience increases in marital satisfaction. This simply means that those bouts of trouble don't last forever. The only difference between couples who remain together and those who don't is that they were able to ride through the rough patches and come out of those situations together with their spouse.

So, what will assist you in coming out of those situations together with a sense of closeness to your spouse? You will need some help, and the Lord is there for you. You will need his strength and guidance. "If you faint in the day of adversity, your strength is small" (Prov. 24: 10). Let me tell you, your strength will be small without the Lord; you are human, and it will be extremely difficult to apply your manmade strength to an uncontrollable variable of an extreme caliber. It's going to require two important fruits of the spirit—longsuffering and joy. Yes, it may seem counterintuitive to say "joy," but the *joy* of the Lord is your strength. In his presence is the fullness of joy. Seek the Lord by spending time in his presence to the point to where the uncontrollable variable isn't dictating your emotions, but where the Lord is guiding and healing your emotions. Remember, the Lord is the only one who has the right to sit on the throne of your emotions. You must remove the uncontrollable variable's influence on the well-being of your heart.

Emotions aren't bad in and of themselves, but being completely ruled by them is walking in the flesh. Connect to your spouse and let your spouse know how you feel about the situation. Get to the point where you can explain the effects of the situation on you and identify the more vulnerable emotions and feelings that may be driving your frustration.

Band together to figure out a strategy to deal with the uncontrollable variable. Seek the Lord and wise counsel, and he will assist you. Get help from others in practical and spiritual ways. If your spouse is at fault for the uncontrollable variable, you must forgive your spouse. Fortunately, we've discussed the steps to the forgiveness process earlier in the book. It's going to be difficult to band together with your spouse to address the uncontrollable variable if you don't forgive your spouse. You will need to forgive yourself. You are human, and you may not have responded initially to the situation in a way in which you would have liked.

Think about the value of your marriage and your unwillingness to sacrifice your marriage due to the uncontrollable variable.

When you come out of the situation, you will have a new per-spective, experience, and deeper appreciation for the Lord and your spouse. Faith, hope, prayer, and godly support will all be great weapons for you during this time. Let the Lord serve as your anchor when the storm of an uncontrollable variable tries to overtake your marriage. Think it not strange concerning the fiery trial that has come to try your marriage. This will require the fruit of the spirit of longsuffering, which means to "endure injury, trouble, or provocation long and patiently. Enduring pain, unhappiness, etc., without complaint."[1]

The important thing to remember when you are weathering the storms of marriage is that you want to interact with your spouse in ways that will enhance the positive culture of your relationship. You don't want to behave in ways that undermine the integrity of your spouse or the integrity of your relationship. You will eventually overcome the uncontrollable variable, and it will not be part of your marriage. However, you are always left with your relationship with your spouse. You want to make sure that the residue of the negative experience doesn't leave your overall relationship in a negative place.

Your Marriage Is So Much Bigger Than the Two of You

Your marriage is about making a positive impact on the larger community—making a positive impact on the current and future generations. I know it's almost cliché; however, it is still worth emphasizing because of its importance. One of the best things you can do for your children is have a healthy marriage and dis-play healthy relationship skills. How many adults do you know who are apprehensive about marriage because they grew up in homes lacking positive examples of a healthy marriage? Now, how many adults do you know who grew up in a home where they saw a positive example of marriage and have this same ap-prehension about marriage? Ample research has demonstrated that children from divorced families are more likely to experience a divorce themselves.[2] Additionally, adult children from divorced families have a lower confidence in their ability to maintain a healthy marriage and tend to have more negative views toward marriage in general when compared to adult children from intact families.[3] The nature and climate of the marriage within a home makes a strong impression on children with regard to their desire to marry and their perceived ability to have a successful marriage. Once again, your marriage is not just about you. The next generation is depending on us to serve as positive examples of marriage.

Marriage Takes Maturity

When it comes to marriage, you are going to have to work your maturity muscle like you are training for a marathon. Immaturity has no place in a marriage. You must man up or woman up. It's required. Choose to be the best version of yourself and find ways to make things work out. Address your bad habits head on now. A great deal of the work you will do in marriage will be on yourself. For the most part, your spouse will not be your problem. You must examine how you may be contributing to problems. When it comes to things you may want to change in your marriage, it will be important for you to consider ways you can change yourself and how that will impact the situation at hand.

OK, now let's talk about emotional maturity. Oftentimes couples come in to see me and they are stuck in their feelings. Like I said before, feelings and emotions are important; however, you don't want to be ruled by them solely. People are usually waiting for a feeling to occur before they want to make changes in their relationship. They ask me, "Hey doc, do you think things will work out?" Well, I don't know; it's up to you. At the time, they are ruled only by their emotions. The emotional climate of the relationship is directing their choices, which ultimately influences their will for the marriage. This is the incorrect order. What do you will to happen in your relationship? That's the important question. What is your will for your marriage? Your will for the relationship should guide and direct your choices and actions, which will inevitably impact the emotional experience of the relationship.

Childishness has no place in marriage, except for when you are having fun! However, things such as pouting, temper tantrums, irresponsibility, and reciprocating bad behavior will eat away at the well-being of your marriage. If you practice childish ways long enough, they will become your default way of handling each other during times of stress, which can undermine your marriage. Make a personal pact with yourself to correct childish behaviors now. "When I was a child, I spake as a child, I understood as a child, I thought as a child; but when I became a man, I put away childish things" (1 Cor. 13:11 KJV).

It's Unrealistic to Believe That You or Your Spouse Won't Change

For anything that is alive and growing, change will occur. Embrace the fact that you will change, and life will bring different circumstances that will require change. Create a new normal.

Your Personal Problems Won't Go Away Because You Get Married

Your issues will either become amplified or they will change. For example, if you have issues with managing money, those issues will become amplified in marriage. Take the time to work on these issues now before you introduce someone else into your life. Now, the reality is that you won't be perfect before marriage, but there are some things you can work on now. It would be helpful to identify at least three areas of personal development that you can work on now before you get married.

The Goal Isn't to Just Fall in Love with Your Spouse

The goal is to fall in love with your spouse repeatedly. Most of us can manage to fall in love with someone once. Consider people you've broken up with in the past. Most would say that they loved those people at the time; however, things didn't work out and you aren't with those people. There must be something more than the initial love and attraction that you have for your spouse. You want your love for your spouse to also grow in grace. This is especially a condition of the heart. You want to condition your heart and mind to look for the best in your spouse and find reasons to fall in love with your spouse. You also want to fall in love with what you are building with your spouse. Fall in love with the projects you are working on together. Fall in love with family you are building. Fall in love with your place and season in marriage.

A helpful way to continuously fall in love with your spouse is by training yourself to see the good in your spouse. Whatever you focus on will be amplified in your life. The same is true with your spouse. Only you have control over what you focus on regarding the characteristics of your spouse. Practice the habit of expressing gratitude to your spouse. We all do better when we are being encouraged rather than discouraged. Research has shown that when we have positive attributions for our partners' behavior, meaning when we see the good intentions of our spouse, this improves satisfaction within the relationship and produces positive interactions in the future.[4]

Gratitude is a seed that reaps positive benefits for both you and your spouse. For example, a five-minute-a-day gratitude journal can improve your overall well-being by ten percent. It also can help you bounce back from stress better. Gratitude also makes us healthier, more likeable, and possibly wealthier.[5] Additionally, it takes maturity to be empathetic at times when you don't feel like it. However, putting yourself in your spouse's shoes is a positive seed and a gift that keeps on giving. It helps to create a positive culture for your marriage and reduce tension on both sides. Gratitude will help build a positive culture and climate for your marriage and your own emotional well-being. Mishaps will occur, and they tend to be weightier than positive experiences. A negative interaction has more of a negative impact on the relationship than a positive interaction has a positive impact on a relationship. What Gottman has found in his research is that there needs to be a five-to-one ratio of five positive interactions to each negative interaction to create a positive culture for the relationship.[6] Gratefulness is the key to unlocking and welcoming more goodness to come into your life. If you aren't in a relationship with a significant other, use this principle on a close friendship or family relationship—it's all transferable to marriage. This positive focus will positively affect your physical health.

You Aren't Entitled to a Good Marriage

You aren't entitled to a good marriage. Just because you are a good person or you are compatible with your spouse, doesn't mean you won't have to work for a good marriage. A good marriage takes work—intentionality, being proactive, prioritizing, and investment. Marriage is a building process; many want the house to be built and fully furnished without putting in the work. You must build the value in your own marriage. You are given raw materials that are valuable, but you need to do the work to put the materials together. Be encouraged in knowing "all hard work leads to profit" (Prov. 14:23a NIV). You can't outsource this work. You must learn and build the skills needed to create the family God created for you. Building a life and family can be a complicated process; however, God will give you wisdom. By wisdom, a house is built, and through understanding, it is established; through knowledge, its rooms are filled with rare and beautiful treasures. (Prov. 24:3 NIV) Even if you prepared and did things God's way prior to marriage, that doesn't entitle you to anything. There is still a breaking and molding process that must take place. It may involve cutting away of some things, hammering some things out, bonding things together, and smoothing out rough patches. People think marriage doesn't work, but the reality is that some are unwilling to put in the work it takes for a marriage to succeed. We want the finished product, but God gives us raw materials and tells us to build.

You may have to get your hands dirty. No work should be beneath you. Rid yourself of titles. What matters is your role of being a husband or wife. Thinking everything should just come easy because you are compatible is an immature mind-set. Understand that building will always be a part of your marriage, even after you have laid the foundation and groundwork and are many years into your marriage. There will always be room for growth, upgrades, maintenance work, and remodeling. Each time you build and add on to your marriage, you increase its value. You are going to have to work on making it work; it doesn't matter how good of a person you are. Just like how you need to qualify for a home, it's helpful to have certain things in order and stored up before you enter marriage. There are certain qualities and experiences that set you up for success in marriage. For men, a clear understanding of your vision, working toward that vision, a clear understanding of your purpose, and strong work ethic; for women, it is a sense of adaptability, an established skillset and training in a specific field, and a clear understanding of your purpose.

You Are Responsible for Your Marriage

Focus on what you can control in your marriage. That's what you are responsible for. You are walking into a covenant, and your contribution is not dependent upon what the other person does. You are held responsible for fulfilling your end of the bargain. Remember, God honors marriage, and he will honor the work you put into your marriage. You must fulfill your part regardless of what the other person does. It's a covenant—not a contract. Now this does exclude the case of abuse.

Your Source of Joy Is Not Your Spouse

You are and always will be responsible for your own joy and happiness. Never put anyone in the seat of controlling your source of joy. We are all people, and we have a hard time enough with trying to keep ourselves in the right mood. It's an illegitimate need and request to have your spouse dictate your joy or happiness. Don't look in the wrong places for your joy. True joy is spending time with the Lord (the joy of the Lord is your strength), making progress on your purpose in life, and having a grateful heart.

You Will Need Jesus

You must develop and continue to develop your relationship with the Lord. He can deal with you during your personal time with him and fulfill you, correct you, and inspire you in the unique ways you need, and you will be receptive. Listen to his voice, he is always calling you to go higher. He is always whispering into your spirit the right thing for you to do that will bring harmony. Listen intently and do whatever he calls for you to do.

Some of the best marital advice I've ever received was to "seek ye first the Kingdom of God and all these things will be added unto you" (Matt. 6:33). I don't think it's by happenstance that I experience the most peace and have a better perspective on my marriage and life when I'm diligently spending quality time with the Lord in prayer and his word. I also see this in therapy. For my believing couples, major infractions and transgressions occur when they have gotten away from spending regular time developing their relationship with the Lord. Your mind-set has such a powerful influence on your marriage, and the enemy wants you to get off in your mind first because he knows that your behaviors and emotions will follow your mind-set. Therefore, we must be diligent in acquiring the mind of Christ on a continual basis. It serves as a repellant for the enemy's seeds to take root in your mind and heart.

You will need godly wisdom to make the proper decisions in marriage. "Through skillful and godly wisdom is a house (a life, a home, a family) built, and by understanding it is established [on a sound and good foundation]. And by knowledge shall its chambers [of every area] be filled with all precious and pleasant riches" (Prov. 24:3-4 AMP). For some situations, you will not have the solution on your own. You will need a route of escape, and it will be imperative that you turn to the one who knows the ending from the beginning.

You Will Face Challenges in Marriage, and It Doesn't Mean That You Did Anything Wrong

I think as Christians, when we have honored God in our courtship process, we expect our marriages to be perfect and without challenges. I know this was true for me—I was like, wait a minute. I'm a nice person who loves the Lord. I remained a virgin until marriage. I had good credit. Wait a minute, Lord. Why am I going through challenges in our marriage? Yep, I was being super self-righteous—forgive me, y'all. God has. You know, we all respect couples who have made it to a fortieth or fiftieth wedding anniversary because we intrinsically know that they weathered some trials together. It's the weathering of the trials and storms that make those marriages valuable and rewarding. The same will be true for your marriage. "Beloved, do not be amazed and bewildered at the fiery ordeal which is taking place to test your quality, as though something strange (unusual and alien to you and your position) were befalling you" (1 Pet. 4:12 AMP). We will experience challenges in all areas of our lives, and marriage is not exempt.

A few things to remember:

- It's a good thing that you have exercised and conditioned your forgiveness muscle because you will also need it in marriage. Your spouse will not be perfect, and you will not be perfect. Be ready to forgive your spouse and yourself. Also, recognize and see the good intentions of your spouse—this will serve as a positive sentiment override. The reality is that all couples go through challenges—both happy and unhappy couples. It's all about how you get through those challenges. Gang up on the challenges instead of each other.
- Complaining will make things worse; search for solutions.
- Make a conscious decision to be the best version of yourself in your marriage.
- A good attitude is easy to have when things are going well, but a good attitude matters most when you go through challenges.

You Must Rid Yourself of a Measuring Stick in Marriage

Your focus shouldn't be on what you are getting out of the relationship/marriage in relation to what you spouse is getting out of the marriage. If you want to have a critical eye on the input and output of the marriage, focus on yourself. What could you be doing that would add value to the relationship and the other person? This is a component of being in a covenant. If you are so focused on not getting the short end of the stick, your end will never be long enough, even if things are going well.

Don't be Ignorant of the Enemy's Devices to Use Relationship Discord to Draw a Wedge in Your Relationship with Christ

You can't have resentment, bitterness and disdain in your heart toward your spouse and expect to be in the clear with the Lord. You can't blatantly do your spouse wrong and think that all is well and good with your relationship with the Lord. This state of unforgiveness and bitterness will affect your relationship with Christ. How can you say you love Christ who you haven't seen, but you don't love your brother who you do see? It's a necessity, and you must die to your flesh.

The enemy wants to create and use a wedge between you and your spouse to create a wedge in your relationship with Christ. The truth of the matter is that you can't have an unforgiving heart toward your spouse and be in right standing with the Lord. This is where the forgiveness muscle comes into play. Communicate effectively about things that may have offended or hurt you. Marriage is the relationship that the word uses to describe Christ's relationship with the church. The enemy understands the significance of marriage, and he wants to dishonor it. You can choose to honor your spouse even when your spouse may be acting dishonorably. Your unconditional love and honor will release favor. Go to the Lord, utilize these times as opportunities to get closer to him and cast your requests on him. He cares about you and your marriage.

Last Words

More than anything, I want you to succeed at marriage and create a legacy of healthy marital functioning for your bloodline. Most importantly, it is the will of God that you prosper in marriage. The advancement of the kingdom is dependent upon us getting the foundation of family right, and the marital relationship is that foundation. You see, God is concerned about the replication of his righteous seed within the earth. That's why he takes the seed of life and places it within the protective covering of a family. A healthy marriage protects and covers its family members. The secure placement of the father within the home is supported by marriage, and the father's primary role is to protect and provide for the family. Marriage is an honorable institution that God highly esteems, and we must also honor what God honors. The unconditional love that is needed for a marriage to thrive is dependent upon a healthy heart, and I hope that your heart is better prepared for marriage after reading this book. I also pray that the information shared in this book has armed you with spiritual and practical tools that you can utilize to make your future or current marriage into the blissful institution that God has designed for your life.

With love,

Dr. Cassandra Bolar

Notes

Introduction

1. Victoria Neufeldt and David B. Guralnik, Webster's New World Dictionary of American English (New York: Prentice Hall, 1994.).

Chapter 1: The Power of Preparation

1. Joshua Medclaf, Chop Wood, Carry Water: How to Fall in Love with the Process of Becoming Great (Morrisville: Lulu Publishing, 2015).
2. "Prepare," Dictionary.com, accessed May 27, 2019, https://www.dictionary.com/browse/prepare.

Chapter 2: Complete Surrender

1. "Surrender," Merriam-Webster, accessed May 27, 2019, https://www.merriam-webster.com/dictionary/surrender.
2. C. M. Dush, C. L. Cohan, and P. R. Amato, "The Relationship between Cohabitation and Marital Quality and Stability: Change across Cohorts?" Journal of Marriage and Family 65 (2003): 539–549, doi:10.1111/j.1741-3737.2003.00539.x.
3. Ruth Umoh, "Why the Secret to Your Success Is Who You Marry," CNN.com, accessed May 27, 2019, https://www.cnbc.com/2017/08/21/why¬the-secret-to-your-success-is-who-you-marry.html.
4. Eleanor Stanford, "13 Questions to Ask before Getting Married," NYTimes.com, accessed May 27, 2019, https://

www.nytimes.com/interactive/2016/03/23/fashion/wed-dings/marriage-questions.html.

5. S. M. Stanley, G. K. Rhoades, and H. J. Markman, "Sliding Versus Deciding: Inertia and the Premarital Cohabitation Effect," Family Relations 55 (2006): 499–509, doi:10.1111/j.1741-3729.2006.00418.x.

6. Kathleen Mullan Harris and J. Richard Udry, National Longitudinal Study of Adolescent to Adult Health (Add Health), 1994-2008 [Public Use]. Ann Arbor, MI: Carolina Population Center, University of North Carolina-Chapel Hill [distribu¬tor], Inter-university Consortium for Political and Social Research [distributor], 2018-08-06. https://doi. org/10.3886/ ICPSR21600.v21

Chapter 3: Examine Your Heart

1. "Examine," Dictionary.com, accessed May 27, 2019, https:// www.dictionary. com/browse/examine?s=t.

2. "What is the Heart?" GotQuestions.org, accessed May 27, 2019, https://www.gotquestions.org/what-is-the-heart. html.

3. "Emotion," Dictionary.com, accessed May 27, 2019, https:// www.dictionary. com/browse/emotion.

4. "Keep," Dictionary.com, accessed May 27, 2019, https:// www.dictionary. com/browse/keep?s=.

5. James Strong, Strong's Exhaustive Concordance of the Bible, updated ed. (Peabody: Hendrickson Publishers, Inc., 2007).

6. "Guard," Dictionary.com, accessed May 27, 2019, https:// www.dictionary. com/browse/guard?s=t.

7. Sue Johnson, Hold Me Tight: Seven Conversations for a Lifetime of Love (Little: Brown Spark, 2008).

8. "Top 10 Causes of Death," World Health Organization, ac-cessed May 27, 2019, https://www.who.int/en/news-room/ fact-sheets/detail/the¬top-10-causes-of-death.

9. "Heart Disease," Mayo Clinic, accessed May 27, 2019, https://www.mayoclinic. org/diseases-conditions/heart-disease/symptoms-causes/syc¬20353118.

Chapter 4: Forgiveness

1. "Forgiveness: Your Health Depends on It," John Hopkins Medicine, accessed May 27, 2019, https://www.hop-kinsmedicine.org/health/ wellness-and-prevention/forgiveness-your-health-depends-on¬it.
2. K. A. Lawler, J. W. Younger, R. L. Piferi, et al., "The Unique Effects of Forgiveness on Health: An Exploration of Pathways," *Journal of Behavioral Medicine* 28 (2005): 157, https://doi.org/10.1007/ s10865-005-3665-2.

Chapter 5: Addressing Fear

1. Kay Hymowitz, Jay Carroll, W. Bradford Wilcox, and Kelleen Kaye, "Knot Yet: The Benefits and Costs of Delayed Marriage in America," accessed May 28, 2019, http://nationalmar¬riageproject.org/wordpress/wp-content/uploads/2013/04/ KnotYet-FinalForWeb-041413.pdf.

Chapter 6: Fullness in Christ: Security, Identity and Purpose

1. Timothy Keller, The Meaning of Marriage: Facing the Complexities of Commitment with the Wisdom of God (London: Penguin Group, 2011).
2. Eli Finkel, The All-or-Nothing Marriage: How the Best Marriages Work (New York: Penguin Random House, 2017).
3. Neufeldt and Guralnik, Webster's New World Dictionary.

Chapter 7: Addressing Selfishness

1. Neufeldt and Guralnik, Webster's New World Dictionary.

Chapter 8: Understanding God's Intent for Marriage

1. Strong, Strong's Exhaustive Concordance.
2. Neufeldt and Guralnik, Webster's New World Dictionary.

3. "Covenant," Theopedia.com, accessed May 28, 2019, https://www.theopedia. com/covenant.

4. "Fruitful," Merriam-Webster, accessed May 28, 2019, https://www.mer¬riam-webster.com/dictionary/fruitful.

5. "Multiply," Merriam-Webster, accessed May 28, 2019, https://www. merriam-webster.com/dictionary/multiply.

6. "Subdue," Merriam-Webster, accessed May 28, 2019, https://www.mer¬riam-webster.com/dictionary/subdue.

7. W. Marsiglio, P. Amato, R. D. Day, and M. E. Lamb, "Scholarship on Fatherhood in the 1990s and Beyond," Journal of Marriage and the Family 62 (2000): 1173–1191.

8. John Eldredge and Stasi Eldredge, Captivating: Unveiling the Mystery of a Woman's Soul (Nashville: Nelson Books, 2005).

9. "Submit," Dictionary.com, accessed May 28, 2019, https://www.dictionary. com/browse/submit?s=t.

Chapter 10: Important Considerations for Choosing a Marital Partner

1. Jon Gordon, The Energy Bus: 10 Rules to Fuel Your Life, Work, and Team with Positive Energy (Hoboken: John Wiley & Sons, Inc., 2007).

2. Keller, The Meaning of Marriage.

1. Ginny Graves, "All about Attraction: What Makes Two People Click? Fall in Love? Keep that Spark Long-Term? Brain Research and Evolutionary Science Are Proving Fascinating Answers," Time, May 3, 2019.

2. John M. Gottman, James Coan, Sybil Carrere, and Catherine Swanson, "Predicting Marital Happiness and Stability from Newlywed Interactions," Journal of Marriage and Family 60, no. 1 (1998): 5–22, doi:10.2307/353438.

Chapter 11: What Happens after Marriage?

1. "Longsuffering," Dictionary.com, accessed May 28, 2019, https://www.dic-tionary.com/browse/longsuffering.

2. P. R. Amato and D. D. DeBoer, "The Transmission of Marital Instability across Generations: Relationship Skills or Commitment to Marriage?" Journal of Marriage and Family 63 (2001): 1038–1051, doi:10.1111/j.1741-3737.2001.01038.x.

3. S. W. Whitton, G. K. Rhoades, S. M. Stanley, and H. J. Markman, "Effects of Parental Divorce on Marital Commitment and Confidence," Journal of Family Psychology 22, no. 5 (2008): 789–793, doi:10.1037/ a0012800.

4. V. Meunier and W. Baker, "Positive Couple Relationships: The Evidence for Long-Lasting Relationship Satisfaction and Happiness," in Positive Relationships, ed. S. Roffey (Dordrecht: Springer Netherlands, 2012).

5. Steve Scott, "31 Benefits of Gratitude You Didn't Know About: How Gratitude Can Change Your Life," accessed May 28, 2019, https://www. happierhuman.com/benefits-of-gratitude/.

6. John Mordechai Gottman and Nan Silver, The Seven Principles for Making Marriage Work (New York: Harmony Books, 2015).